Memories
of
Norwich

Part of the
Memories
series

The Publishers would like to thank the following companies for supporting the production of this book

Main Sponsor
RG Carter Group

Anglia Square Shopping Centre

MF Barnwell & Sons

The Butcher Group

Bowhill & Elliot (East Anglia) Limited

City College Norwich

T Gill & Son (Norwich) Limited

GW Gooch & Sons Limited

Hamilton Acorn Limited

Edward Hines (Engineers) Limited

The Howes Group

The Holden Group

Lambert Scott Innes

Loose's Limited

Norwich Union plc

H Smith & Sons (Honingham) Limited

RC Snelling Limited

First published in Great Britain by True North Books Limited
Units 3 - 5 Heathfield Industrial Park
Elland West Yorkshire
HX5 9AE
Tel. 01422 377977
© Copyright: True North Books Limited 1999

ISBN 1 900463 73 3

Text, design and origination by True North Books Limited
Printed and bound by The Amadeus Press Limited

Memories are made of this

Memories. We all have them; some good, some bad, but our memories of the city we grew up in are usually tucked away in a very special place in our minds. The best are usually connected with our childhood and youth, when we longed to be grown up and paid no attention to adults who told us to enjoy being young, as these were the best years of our lives. We look back now and realise that they were right.

So many memories - perhaps of the war and rationing, perhaps of parades, celebrations and Royal visits. And so many changes; one-way traffic systems and pedestrianisation.

New trends in shopping that led to the very first self-serve stores being opened.

Through the bad times and the good, however, Norwich not only survived but prospered. We have only to look at the city as it is today, with its finest remaining buildings now restored to their full glory, and the traditional tourist attractions now complemented by up-to-the-minute facilities, to see what progress has been realised and what achievements have been made over the last 50 years. Norwich has a history to be proud of - but more importantly, a great future to look forward to, into the new millennium and beyond.

Contents

Section one

Around the city centre

•

Section two

High days and holidays

•

Section three

On the home front

•

Section four

Events & occasions

•

Section five

Changing city

•

Section six

On the move

•

Section seven

Shopping spree

•

Section eight

At work

Around the city centre

It's another miserable day as people huddle to do their shopping under whatever shelter they can find from the rain that has been coming down all day. It would be all too easy to step out into the road, hunched up against the elements, whether the traffic signal said 'Don't cross' or not. An increase in traffic around the city centre was becoming a problem. As the austere 1950s were left behind, money and hire purchase for luxury items, like the motor car, were becoming more available. The grace of London Street is well set off by the smooth lines of the Jaguar easing its way towards us. Somehow, the 'Jag' epitomises all that is good and stylish in the best of British engineering. The first model was produced in 1936 by SS

Cars and was given a name that suggests speed and sleek power. The company, not surprisingly, was renamed in 1945 to avoid reminding us all of Hitler's troopers. It took on the name of its most successful model. Branching out into motor sport, the Jaguar had great success in sports car racing and rallying in the 1950s. So much so, it bought out the mighty Daimler in 1960, not long before this photograph was taken. Later mergers saw it come under the umbrella of British Leyland. This car is on the right street for smartness. Buildings like Jarrold's store and George Skipper's offices were excellent examples of Edwardian building. Skipper was the artistic brain behind many Norfolk buildings, including Norwich's Royal Arcade.

A glance at the 1930s

WHAT'S ON?

In this heyday of the cinema, horrified audiences were left gasping at the sight of Fay Wray in the clutches of the giant ape in the film 'King Kong', released in 1933. Very different but just as gripping was the gutsy 1939 American Civil War romance 'Gone with the Wind'. Gable's parting words, 'Frankly, my dear, I don't give a damn' went down in history.

GETTING AROUND

At the beginning of the decade many believed that the airship was the transport of the future. The R101 airship, however, loaded with thousands of cubic metres of hydrogen, crashed in France on its maiden flight in 1930. Forty-eight passengers and crew lost their lives. In 1937 the Hindenburg burst into flames - the entire disaster caught on camera and described by a distraught reporter. The days of the airship were numbered.

SPORTING CHANCE

The black American Jesse Owens won a brilliant four world records in the 1936 Olympic Games in Berlin, thumbing the nose to Adolph Hitler's dreams of Aryan superiority. In a petty display Hitler walked out of the stadium and 'took his bat home'; later he refused to have his photograph taken with the victorious Owens.

Deep into the summer of 1972, this is an aerial shot taken in August. The once proud Colegate runs roughly across the centre of the picture, from Magdalen Street to Coslany Street. Despite being swallowed up in this photograph, down at ground level it has the appearance of being one of the city's richest architectural areas. This is especially true of the Thorp chapel to St Clement's church district. There were many Georgian houses that were

connected with the great 18th century families. One example is Bacon House. Henry Bacon was the mayor from 1557 to 1566. The scene along Colegate changed a few years after the time this scene recalls. Renovation of the area was so successful that it carried off the 1975 award for European Architectural Heritage. Development into the 1980s brought the imaginative conversion of the Norvic shoe factory. It was one of the earliest and largest of its type in the country. The inner ring road, heading left, acts as a feeder to all parts of the city. The various roundabouts and junctions on the route throw traffic into and out from the centre, depending on the flow of the one way system. You can usually tell a driver who is visiting for the first time. He is the one you have seen going round 10 minutes ago, continually looking left. That puzzled look has stayed there the whole time. The problem is, once he has got in, will he ever be able to get the right way out again?

Bottom: You need a good head for heights to be a photographer. This one was standing at the top of the Norwich Union building and looking out across Timberhill. Once known as Durnsdale, as might be guessed from its present name, the land was once used as a timber market. This was particularly important in the 14th century, during the reign of Edward III. The Franciscan friars were active around here from the 13th century. Despite much damage being caused in the bombing raid of 27 June 1942, you can still find a mix of ages and styles in the variety of little shops there to-day. One of the entrances to the Castle Mall shopping complex is from Timberhill. It wasn't always such a gentle place to stroll along. Gangs of ruffians and groups of drunkards used to make the area one to steer clear of. Two hundred years ago it was referred to as Blood and Guts Alley. Men who would crack open your head for a few pence or the price of a night's drinking toured, looking for a 'mark'. If you were it, then showing a clean set of heels was your best defence. As in the popular saying, it was a poor pair of legs that would see a body abused. Many of those who died in the City Gaol were buried in the churchyard of St John Timberhill. It is ironic if it was on Timberhill that they had started the mischief that brought them to prison, because they were to return to the scene of their misdeeds forever.

Right: Around Norwich's Anglican Cathedral is Cathedral Close. It is one of the largest in England and is a quiet and serene enclosure. The houses in the Upper Close are mainly given over to offices. Those in the Lower Close are chiefly residential. Many of the other buildings form part of the King Edward VI (Norwich) School. A statue to Admiral Lord Nelson, the hero of Trafalgar and other sea battles, stands here. He was once a pupil at Norwich School. Two tremendous gateways lead into the Close from Tombland.

At one end is the Erpingham Gate, donated by Sir Thomas a few years after his success as at the 1415 Battle of Agincourt. The gate here is St Ethelbert Gate. It is the main roadway into the Close. Just inside the gate there was once a church dedicated to St Ethelbert. It was destroyed in the riots of 1272. As a penance for the sins of their fellows, local people rebuilt this gate and gave it the name of the saint whose memory had been so tarnished. The chapel above the gateway echoes to the strains of young voices and their instruments. It is the King Edward School music room. Listen carefully and perhaps you can hear the boys and girls practising their Glorias and chants. Students from the school sing in the Cathedral choir every day during term time.

Above: Exchange Street was the first new street to be built since Norman times. Over seven centuries had gone by without the need for new thoroughfares. Even to-day, there is plenty of evidence in the narrow streets and nooks and crannies of the city of those medieval days. It was in 1829 that Exchange Street was born and provided a final city centre link with the coaching yard of the Tuns Inn. Seeing the light of day as Post Office Street, as the head post office was here, it was renamed in honour of the Corn Exchange. This exchange was on Sir Benjamin Wrench's Court and is now part of the large Jarrold's store. The Corn Exchange, which had been established in 1861, was demolished in 1964 and the Jarrold's despatch department covers the site. Thorn's Ironmongers and Toolmerchants survives into the 21st century. The shop hasn't changed much. The signwriting style may have altered, but, inside, it's business as usual. Around here, though, there has been some development from the late 60s. Across, on the other side of the street corner, is 24 Exchange Street. Waltzes, the quickstep and the foxtrot were on offer in the first floor dance studio. This building is now the Health Information Centre. Looking carefully at the relief work above the door, the designs of bunches of grapes can be made out. There used to be quite a number of vintners and wine and spirits stores along Exchange Street. So many, in fact, that older locals once called it 'Boozers' Row'. Fortunately, the name didn't stick.

A glance at the 1930s

HOT OFF THE PRESS

The years of the 1930s saw Adolph Hitler's sickening anti-Jewish campaign echoed in the streets of Britain. On 19th October 1936 Oswald Mosley's 7,000-strong British Union of Fascists clashed head on with thousands of Jews and Communists in London, resulting in 80 people being injured in the ensuing battle. Mosley and his 'blackshirts' later rampaged through the streets beating up Jews and smashing the windows of their businesses.
A dark day in our country's history.

THE WORLD AT LARGE

In India, Gandhi's peaceful protests against British rule were gathering momentum. The Salt Laws were a great bone of contention: forced to buy salt from the British government, thousands of protestors marched to the salt works, intending to take it over in the name of the Indian people. Policemen and guards attacked the marchers, but not one of them fought back. Gandhi, who earned for himself the name 'Mahatma' - Great Soul - was assassinated in 1948.

ROYAL WATCH

The talking point of the early 1930s was the affair of the Prince of Wales, who later became King Edward VIII, and American divorcee Wallis Simpson. Faced with a choice, Edward gave up his throne for 'the woman I love' and spent the remainder of his life in exile. Many supported him, though they might not have been as keen to do so if they had been aware of his Nazi sympathies, kept strictly under wraps at the time.

Any moment now and an accordion player will come along. Maybe we'll see a chap on a bicycle with a string of onions over his shoulder. Surely this is the French capital, with its streetside cafés? If they were sipping a cognac and dragging on a Gauloise it would identify the spot. As it is only a cup of Typhoo and an Embassy filter we'll have to accept that this bright day is captured on London Street. Still, the accordion might come, if not the onion seller.

Especially on Saturdays, street entertainers entertain the passers-by. It's not just the usual trumpeter or guitarist, plus dog, but a variety of musicians, from pan pipe players to string quartets and skiffle groups. For the last 35 years Norwich folk have walked the paved streets as a matter of practice, forgetting the car exhaust fumes of other parts of the city. Our little group at the table can chat without shouting against the noise or splut-tering through the polluted emissions. It's a much more civilised way to shop, relax and enjoy the city. Why didn't we think of it before? Before, that is, we allowed the motor car to dominate our lives and remove the pleasure that taking your time can bring. When elevenses is over, why not pop into the florist for a plant for Auntie Ethel? There are even a few minutes spare so that a card can be written with a personal and thoughtful message.

Above: The view is from Gentleman's Walk, across the northern edge of Market Pace, looking west. Standing proudly to the right of the City Hall, the stone and flint of the Guildhall reminds us that the history of medieval Norwich is our heritage. The building is our main link with the city affairs of long ago. Whilst it is now the local tourist information centre, for centuries the Guildhall was the hub of city government. It also housed the assize courts and was home to the magistrates' court until 1986. In the late 19th century the south wing was used as a police station. The architecture is a joy to behold. The public clock, erected by Alderman Woodcock, is just one of the striking features. The Bassingham Gate was brought specially from London. Inside no-one can fail to be impressed by the carved Tudor ceiling of the old council chamber or the 15th century stained glass window. It was in this building in 1549 that the rebel Robert Kett was held before his execution at the castle. He and his brother had led a revolt over land enclosures. They camped out on Mousehold Heath and marched on the city. Captured by the King's forces, the Guildhall was Kett's home for only a short time before the axe fell. This peasants' revolt had been against unpopular measures introduced across the country by the Lord Protector, Edward Seymour, the Duke of Somerset. It was ironic that Somerset, himself, was executed for treason in 1552.

Above right: A damp and blustery day has come to harass the shoppers on Brigg Street, heading for the Universal Stores at the top of the picture. In Charles II's day it was called Brigg's Lane. It had been named after Augustus Brigg. He was a born survivor. Not many could say that in the 17th century and its days of rebellion and civil war. He, unlike many of his fellow citizens in Norwich, was a staunch Royalist. He was a mayor and Member of

Parliament both before and after the Restoration. The street that bore his name was widened around 1900 to allow trams to run along it. Linking the Haymarket with Rampant Horse Street, it is now pedestrianised. The pavements here have always been thronged with shoppers, as it is one of the main concentrations of a variety of retail outlets in the city. The cycle shop and the butcher sit happily side by side. The woman in the utilitarian plastic rain hood is more likely to be crossing the road for a pound of sausages than a drop-handle Raleigh racer, but you never know. The awnings were first provided to protect goods from the sunlight, but canny shopkeepers soon realised that they were useful in bad weather as well. They provided a shelter from the rain. This wasn't a charitable move. When shoppers gathered under the awning to escape the showers, they were prey to the attractions on display. You can just imagine Jean Alexander as TV's Auntie Wainwright in 'Last of the summer wine' rubbing her hands in glee at such a prospect.

Bridewell Alley leads away from the centre towards St Andrew's Church. The women walking towards us are lost in earnest conversation. Perhaps they are American tourists. It was said that Abraham Lincoln's ancestors worshipped at this church. Many visitors from our former colony across the Atlantic came to see the place where the great man's forebears might have prayed. Whilst there is no definite proof that this was the case, don't tell the Yanks. Let them spend their dollars here. The women are more likely to be locals. There isn't a camera between them. The old chap on the left is definitely one of ours. He looks at home. Bridewell is the home of one of Norwich's best museums. Since 1925 it has been home to a history of local industry and craft. Farm techniques, boot and shoe making, textiles, metal working and fine flint building are all displayed here. You can find out about the art of making everything from chocolate to shawls, from steam engines to clocks. In the 1783 Norwich Directory it was described as 'a large and curious building, built of square flint and stone'. When that was written, the Bridewell was a prison. The original St Bride's Well was a prison in London. The Norwich version housed petty offenders, tramps and beggars. Perhaps that is why these women are on the move. They don't want to be detained as vagrants. They'd better tell old 'pop' on the corner. We don't want to see him getting his collar felt.

Some fuddy-duddies thought that the paving of London Street meant that it had lost its narrow, intimate character. They even said it was like a precinct. Not when looked at from here. From his position above, the cameraman has caught the busy, but smart, personality of one of the city's smarter shopping areas. The bow of the building line, the power of the old architecture and the gentle atmosphere of the shops made being out and about in 1969 a pleasurable experience. We had lived through a decade of changing attitudes. The young had become a power in the land, with money in their pocket and a voice to be listened to. Peace and love, not war; it was a time of social conscience. As Bob Dylan sang to us, 'The times they were a-changing.' Fashions altered dramatically. Men entered the 60s with Brylcreemed hair, cut short or swept back to a DA. Their suits were navy blue. Women went out, their permanently waved hair under headscarves and wearing cotton mid-calf prints. Examine the scene below and some of the young men have no ears! If they have, they are well hidden under flowing locks. Some are even wearing coloured shirts and pale trousers. There's hardly a hat to be seen as the women have thrown them away along with their bras in those times of liberation. Hemlines went up and the curtain came down on an era when you were supposed to know your place. It was to become what you could make of it.

Above: *At last it is ready. Curl's department store has reopened. It stands majestically on the corner of Rampant Horse Street and Red Lion Street. The contractor has done a fine job. The Edwardian feel to the frontage is attractive. It is certain that Prince Charles would not have considered this to be one of the architectural carbuncles he criticised elsewhere. The bobby on point duty is rather under employed. As there are not many people or much traffic about, it must be early morning. Give it time. The morning rush will soon be upon him. Then those white armbands will leap into action. In the 50s and 60s the bobby in his box at the crossroads was a familiar sight. His gestures were dramatic. There was a sense of power as that right arm raised heavenwards. All movement to the front of him stopped immediately. Then, with one sweeping movement of his left arm across him, everything to that side moved on as one. He did not need the whistles and klaxons of the Latin militia or French gendarme. He was British. He could say it all with one imperious movement. What was a puzzle was how he got in or out of his box. Did some celestial crane lift him in or was he winched down from a helicopter? No-one knows. It was just one of life's little mysteries. To-day he has been replaced at the country's crossroads by the mini roundabout. Is nothing sacred?*

High days and holidays

'Anyone for checkers?' If you heard that cry in February 1952, it wasn't Winston Churchill asking people away to his country retreat. The sound would have been heard in St Clement'' vicarage. It is the name that British call draughts. This was the home of the Anglo-American club. The female NCO looks a bit snooty. She has just seen a good move to open up the board and get a crown for one of the pieces. If the player about to play his move does not take that next piece he will be huffed. Only serious students of the game would follow this! These were the days of Brylcreemed hair and Denis Compton advertising the hair adornment. This was proper man's stuff. How could a Manchester United footballer in a sarong be as acceptable advertising the 1999 version of the product? The men feeding coins into the jukebox were searching for popular hits of the day. A juke was really a brothel, but we hope the vicar didn't know! It was too early for rock and roll, but jive and jitterbug records would be available. There might be a song by the Andrews Sisters who had advised us during the war not to sit under apple trees without them. They wouldn't be around much longer as they split up the following year. Other popular American singers of the time were Jo Stafford, Kay Starr and the 'unforgettable' Nat King Cole. By the way, of course we know that the PM would have been off to Chequers.

Below: What hopes and dreams lie shattered here? It was not just the destruction of the buildings that hurt. We could defy the Nazis and rebuild what they had knocked down. But, could we replace and rekindle that ray of hope and optimism surrounding a new business that had just begun or the first house of the newlywed that had been blitzed. Not just bricks and mortar had been shattered, for some of us it was our dreams. They were more fragile than the concrete that had come crashing down around our ears. The 'nó entry' sign on the left did not mean much to the pilots who brought Goering's bombs to us. As they entered, some of our aspirations exited. We could join in the concerts and the dancing of June's Norwich Festival, but would we ever waltz as hopefully again? Some people clustered happily in the doorway of Paige's shop. However, it is those who are passing by the fence who seem to share the emptiness of the day. Their heads are carefully

turned away from the scene of death and destruction alongside them. They do not want to be reminded. Who can blame them? One woman has her head bowed low as the weight of the memory of those harrowing times falls upon her. She is dressed in black. Perhaps her burden is made the heavier by the loss of loved ones.

Bottom: You were never off duty if you were a member of any of the civil defence movements. An emergency was just around the corner, waiting to happen. Even so, there was no need to wait for the call in uncomfortable surroundings. The rest and recreation area of the headquarters building was there for a refreshing cuppa or a thumb through the pages of Woman's Own, or whatever else was lying about. The female members were just as valued as their male counterparts and it was no surprise to see them sharing the facilities here. It might have been

pushing emancipation too far if one of the ladies put a shilling down on the corner of the billiard table. This was still a man's domain and women were thought of as potential cloth rippers if they ever picked up a cue. That's an attitude that has changed hardly at all. Few clubs in 1999 give women the opportunity to play. The prize money for their world championship is only around £1,000, compared with a six figure sum for the men. The two chaps at the top of the picture couldn't care less about equality or the world of the professional player. They've got a few more cannons to make and the odd screw back with check side to play before this game of billiards is through. But if this in-off is successful, it's a big step towards the other bloke paying for the light meter.

It is hard to believe that this photograph is almost 50 years old. The Tombland Fair - an annual event held each Easter - was eagerly awaited by young and old alike. The fair is thought to date from pre-Norman times, and was held on an area of land where previously a cattle market took place. The origins of the fair were related to trade - thousands of people being drawn to it from all over the county. In later years the fair remained, but simply as a pleasure-related event. Those old enough to remember the fair may recall the wall of sound, vivid colours and enticing calls from the stall holders, not to mention the growl of the generators and the smell of their exhaust fumes - sharply contrasting with the sweet aroma of candyfloss and toffee apples. Happy days indeed!

It was all hands to the pump on the nights of 29/30 April 1942. Civil Defence members, the police force, ambulance services, air raid wardens, the WVS and all manner of official and voluntary groups were stretched to the limit on those nights. The worst of the Blitz had hit the city. None was more hard pressed than the National Fire Service. Water mains had ruptured and it was the most difficult of jobs to find enough serviceable hydrants to keep going, but they did. Water was even pumped from nearby rivers and reservoirs, so urgent and demanding was the need. Support from the Auxiliary Fire Service was much appreciated. It pressed into service some of the converted saloon cars it had at its Bethel Street HQ. Even so, Norwich burned and smouldered for days afterwards. Bunting's department store on Rampant Horse Street was one of many fine businesses and buildings to be gutted. Eventually, it would come back to life as Curl's and, later still, Debenham's. Both these stores kept faith with the past. In the meantime, the NAAFI set up a club on this site. The Navy, Army and Air Force Institute, to give it the official title, set up many such clubs and centres across the nation for the troops. As well as providing a bar, a café and a place to lounge about for a few hours away from the strain of the war, performers from ENSA (Entertainments National Service Association) would entertain. Although the TV sitcom 'It ain't half hot mum' somewhat mocked this organisation, service men and women were grateful for the escape from reality it gave.

On the home front

Below: The civil defence headquarters were situated on Market Avenue. There is quite a military feel to this part of Norwich. The Avenue is behind the castle and is home to the Shirehall and Norfolk Regimental Museum. A war memorial stands on the northern end of Market Avenue and to the south was the Drill Hall where the Territorial Army later met. Sitting in the hangar garage, ready to race into action, these vehicles owe their existence to man's inability to live together peacefully. It was in 1936, with the rumbling of war machines across Europe, that the first Air Raid Protection committees were first set up. There was civil war in Spain, Mussolini's forces had invaded Abyssinia and Hitler had mobilised and entered the Rhineland, defying the Treaty of Versailles. Although there was a temporary lull in 1938, when Mr Chamberlain brought his useless bit of paper back from Berlin, Britain started to prepare for war. The wardens' service gave out 126,000 gas masks or respirators, as they were properly known. Air raid shelters to house 17,000 had been prepared by the time war broke out. This had risen to 122,000 by 1942, when the night skies above Norwich would be filled with the fiery rain of death from high explosive bombs and incendiaries. The civil defence corps risked life and limb in assisting the fire services and pulling people from piles of rubble as buildings crashed around them. Even after the war, the vehicles pictured here would be plunged into action in times of local disaster. Major floods and other incidents would see them roll out their emergency equipment to build temporary housing, shore up damaged homes or premises and help co-ordinate rescues.

A glance at the 1930s

MELODY MAKERS

Throughout the 1930s a young American trombonist called Glenn Miller was making his mark in the world of music. By 1939 the Glenn Miller sound was a clear leader in the field; his clean-cut, meticulously executed arrangements of numbers such as 'A String of Pearls' and 'Moonlight Serenade' brought him fame across the world as a big-band leader. During a flight to England from Paris in 1944 Miller's plane disappeared; no wreckage was ever found.

INVENTION AND TECHNOLOGY

With no driving tests or speed restrictions, 120,000 people were killed on the roads in Britain between the two world wars. In 1934 a Halifax man, Percy Shaw, invented a safety device destined to become familiar the world over: reflecting roadstuds. In dark or foggy conditions the studs that reflected light from the car's headlights kept traffic on the 'straight and narrow' and must over the years have saved many lives.

SCIENCE AND DISCOVERY

By observing the heavens, astronomers had long believed that there in the constellation of Gemini lay a new planet, so far undiscovered. They began to search for the elusive planet, and a special astronomical camera was built for the purpose. The planet Pluto was discovered by amateur astronomer Clyde Tombaugh in 1930, less than a year later.

Above: The cooker and boiler are taking shape. It is hard, backbreaking work, but the rewards of this training exercise at Oulton will come in the field. Knowing how to build a feeding station from scratch will be second nature to these WVS members by then. The pipe on this one will be topped off with the familiar cap on its chimney, similar to the old Soyer boiler. Forms of boilers used on other days included ones with such names as the 'dustbin' boiler. That description told you exactly what you could use as an alternative to the purpose-built model. To add spice to this training exercise, it was run on a competitive basis. Teams met the 'Challenge' of building and firing the cooker. Members had to answer questions on emergency feeding procedure. The winning team would progress to the next round of the knockout competition, to be held two months later at Cambridge on 7 July 1956. The Yarmouth team got their cooker up and running first. When the oral test points were added, it had scored 75. However, Norwich outscored it with 82, but the overall winner was the Norfolk County team that rattled up 84 points. Never mind, it was still a rewarding day. New friends had been made, amongst the rivalries, and skills fine tuned. The real winners of the Emergency Feeding competition would be the general public who would benefit if it had to call on the WVS for help.

Right: The Oulton Centre in East Suffolk was used as the Civil Defence Training Centre in its early years. In this 1956 training exercise, the women of the WVS have made a start on something that will be more than a humble 'barbie'. At the moment you could pop a few skewers on top and feed the family with rolls of bacon and spiked sausage. The plan was for something grander. From this humble beginning, one of a number of ovens and cooking ranges would grow. They would be able to heat food for dozens of people at a time. The WVS regarded itself as an active emergency service and doers not airy-fairy thinkers filled its ranks. In 1953, the Service had given valuable support in helping the flood victims along the East Coast. Conditions were particularly bad around Yarmouth when the Yare broke its banks down river at Galston. Because of the nature of the coastline and the low-lying hinterland, flood alerts have been a continuing saga in the life of the WVS/WRVS. Especially during the winter, the volunteers seem to be hopping from one tide to the next. Sometimes it is not just water that is brought in on the tide. In 1999, an unexploded mine was washed up on the beach at Mundesley, just down the coast from Cromer. The WRVS was put on standby should evacuation have been necessary. It is on such occasions that the training exercises bear fruit.

You did not join the Women's Voluntary Service and expect to keep your hands clean. No manicure and hand beauty treatment for these ladies of the Yarmouth team. Mucking in together was never a truer statement when applied to them. Mrs R Parker, Mrs A Bowen, Mrs M Cullington and Mrs CR Wiliams demonstrate the qualities of teamwork. They are on the Norfolk Exercise Challenge, a practical, competitive exercise in sharpening their skills. This one was held on 12 May 1956. The object was to build an open air stove and Soyer-type boiler from the provided materials, making it similar to those that were used in the field. With their know-how tested under the simulated conditions of a disaster response, they would feel all the more capable when providing support in a real emergency. Within a short time these ladies would have a series of feeding stations ready to dispense hot food to give to victims of tragedies and the rescue teams who had descended on the incident. You don't make an omelette without cracking eggs any more than you erect a range from bricks, mud, drainpipes and grilles without breaking a fingernail or two. The members of the Norfolk WVS have been seen supporting their fellow defence and rescue teams at every major local incident since they were formed. Relief hasn't stopped at the county border, support being given to other counties in times of their great needs.

Below: This Cambridge group of WVS members is one of the Food Flying Squads that mobilised quickly in response to any major incident or disaster where their response and support skills could be used. It is pictured at the Emergency Feeding Station Training Centre at Diss on 13 July 1955. From the early days of its work in 1938, women flocked to join to be of service. 'What can you do?' asked ARP posters at the beginning of the war. More women than men responded by volunteering their services as Air Raid Wardens. However, given little to do, they drifted off. Happily, many were then recruited by the WVS. The Queen took an interest, becoming president at the outbreak of the war. Her daughter, Elizabeth II, gave the crown's seal of approval in 1966 when the service became the Women's Royal Voluntary Service. These days the 'W' is played down, as over 10 per cent of members are male. The work goes on for the local teams, and not just around Norwich. In 1988 they answered the call at Lockerbie, in the aftermath of the terrorist attack that brought down an airliner on the Scottish town, killing 270 people. For three weeks the WRVS served 3,000 meals a day to those involved in the investigations and clearing up. A relative centre, as a form of comfort scheme, was set up at Hillsborough where 96 spectators died at a football match in 1989.

Bottom: The Coronation of Queen Elizabeth II and Stanley Matthews getting his only FA Cup winner's medal are two of the main events of 1953 for most English people. Norfolk and East Coast dwellers remember it for another reason. It was the year of the great floods. Over the years we have suffered from the ravages of the sea and flooding rivers, but few incidents can compare with 3 February, that year. Sea defences collapsed from Lincolnshire to Kent as hurricanes drove high tides across the barriers. The River Yare broke its banks and the WVS moved into action, setting up feeding stations for the emergency services and for the homeless who were billeted in church halls and schoolrooms. Appeals for clothing were made as people had lost so much to the floodwaters. The response was excellent, but it fell to the WVS to organise the sorting and distribution of tons of garments. The vicar and his curate have come with their shopping list of items that are needed in their flock. This experienced volunteer will put them straight. Her knowledge and training will help her supply just what they really need to get people through the crisis. Some 300 poor souls lost their lives in the disaster, over 60 of these being in Norfolk. They included 12 American servicemen drowned near Hunstanton. It was in such times that the professionalism of the members of the Women's Voluntary Service shone out like a beacon, bless them.

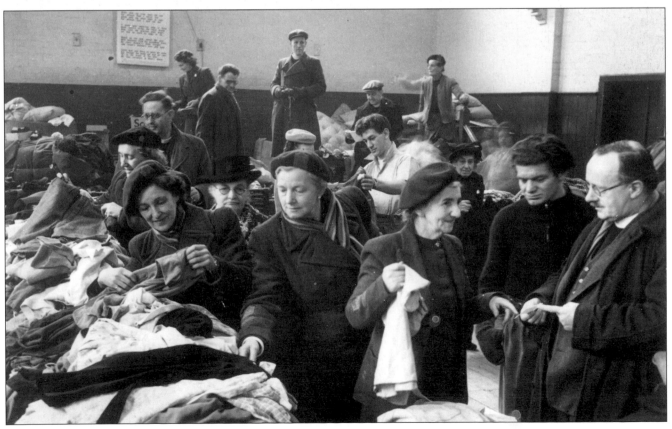

Events & occasions

A glance at the 1940s

WHAT'S ON?
In wartime Britain few families were without a wireless set. It was the most popular form of entertainment, and programmes such as ITMA, Music While You Work and Mrs Dale's Diary provided the people with an escape from the harsh realities of bombing raids and ration books. In 1946 the BBC introduced the Light Programme, the Home Service and the Third Programme, which gave audiences a wider choice of listening.

GETTING AROUND
October 1948 saw the production of Britain's first new car designs since before the war. The Morris Minor was destined for fame as one of the most popular family cars, while the four-wheel-drive Land Rover answered the need for a British-made off-road vehicle. The country was deeply in the red, however, because of overseas debts incurred during the war. The post-war export drive that followed meant that British drivers had a long wait for their own new car.

SPORTING CHANCE
American World Heavyweight Boxing Champion Joe Louis, who first took the title back in 1937, ruled the world of boxing during, making a name for himself 1940s as unbeatable. Time after time he successfully defended his title against all comers, finally retiring in 1948 after fighting an amazing 25 title bouts throughout his boxing career. Louis died in 1981 at the age of 67.

Below: The WVS had come along way from its humble origins as a modest part of the country's Civil Defence. With a driving force such as Lady Stella Reading as the chairman and figurehead, it was not long before the movement had developed its own identity. In late 1951, she is pictured on the right with the American ambassador's wife, Mrs Gifford. On a museum visit, the curator, Mr Clark, is showing them round. Lady Reading had been at the heart of the Personal Service League of the early 30s that helped families adversely affected by the depression years. Born Stella Charnaud, in 1894, in Constantinople, she brought her cosmopolitan, but social, conscience to the front line of helping the unfortunate. After her husband's death in 1935, she immersed herself in charitable projects. The WVS was formed in 1938 and Lady Reading became its first chairman. Recognising that war was coming, the WVS organised first aid and gas defence classes for civilians. These women ran trolley shops in hospitals and cared for the relatives of men who were on the danger list. Their later work in wartime would see a number of them appear on the same danger list. The first bomb that fell on Britain landed on a WVS house in the Orkneys in February 1940! One member single-handedly captured a German parachutist in Yorkshire. She led him, on the end of her pitchfork, to the local police station where the flier was happy to be locked up in safety.

Above: This gathering took place on Unthank Rd. The road has a developing history of its own shown in the architecture. As you travel its length the housing styles move from Georgian to Victorian and through from Edwardian to the 1930s. Many of the larger houses have been turned into student quarters. Collected there in this photograph are some of the Cavell nurses from the nurses' home that was near the Maids' Head Hotel, one of the country's oldest inns. Younger readers might need to be reminded of the selfless heroism of the woman whose name inspired those pictured here. Edith Cavell was born in Swardeston in 1865, becoming a nurse at the age of 30. As matron of the Berkendael Institute in Brussels, she greatly improved nursing standards. When Germany occupied Belgium at the beginning of the Great War of 1914-18, she became involved in an underground group that helped Allied soldiers reach the neutral Netherlands. The soldiers were sheltered at the Institute, which had become a Red Cross hospital, and given money and guides to take them across the border. Over 200 men were helped. She and several others were arrested in August 1915. Despite the efforts of American and Spanish ministers, she was shot by a firing squad on 12 October, two months short of her 50th birthday. Queen Alexandra opened a memorial to her, in front of the Maids' Head, on the third anniversary of her death. Thousands flocked to the scene to pay their own tributes. The next year her body was exhumed from the Belgian rifle range where it had lain. After a special memorial service in Westminster Abbey, she found her final resting place at Life's Green, near the Cathedral.

Top: Now let's see if you are going to glow in the dark. The lad having his hand checked for radioactivity looks anxious. Is the geiger counter going to crackle and give off a frighteningly high reading? There's really nothing to worry about, because it's only a civil defence demonstration and exhibition. The corps was on a membership drive. At the same time it was trying to raise the awareness of the general public. It was a case of catch them young. Gadgets fascinated all little lads. To see this sort of demonstration with its literal hands-on experience attracted them like moths to the flame. The French scientist Becquerel first reported the existence of radioactivity in 1896, but the release of nuclear energy wasn't realised until during the Second World War. After the bombing of Hiroshima and Nagasaki the western world became uneasy about the dangers of radiation. The cold war days of the 1960s made us all mindful of what might happen if missiles were launched. These were the days of four-minute warnings and fall-out shelters. The civil defence would play a major role in organising evacuation and good order, should the unthinkable happen. So, on this recruitment day, tables and display stands were set out in St Andrew's Hall. It had been a huge church and a Dominican friary was established inside it in 1471. By the early 19th century it had become Norwich's main concert hall, hosting one of England's oldest music festivals, the Norwich and Norfolk Triennial. A large organ separates the hall from Blackfriars' Hall, so named because of the colour of the habits the old friars used to wear.

America kept a heavy presence in Europe after World War II. In part it was to oversee the peacetime activities of West Germany, but also to guard against the territorial ambitions of the communist Soviet Union. By the 1950s there were married quarters on the US air bases and servicemen's wives had come out to join them. They were keen to fit into Norfolk society and show appreciation for the welcome that their men had received from the local population. This was one of the tea parties the wives threw at Sculthorpe, near Fakenham. Name badges were worn to help break the ice and cut down on the need for introductions. The elegant American in the centre could have plucked from the pages of Vogue or Harper's Bazaar. Chic isn't the word. No wonder the woman with the glasses is giving her the once-over. In the austerity of the first decade after the war, we had to ration our clothing. She has walked straight out of the haute couture house. The handbag, that necessary fashion item, perfectly sets off the little black number she is wearing. The lovely wavy hair under the oh so pert little hat is in sharp contrast to the tight perms of those around her. Of course, being every inch a lady, the white gloves stay firmly in place as she delicately balances the teacup. Her fellow countrywoman, on the left, is a much raunchier model, with her style of clothing and daring to smoke in public.

Right: The official opening of the Anglo-American club attracted many local and public bigwigs to the ceremony. It was of great interest to both the British and the Americans. Lady Reading came to mark the occasion and the ever faithful British bobby was on hand to keep the crowds in check and help the dignitaries move smoothly towards the opening ceremony. In Norfolk we had become used to seeing hordes of our allies around for ages. There were 18 American air bases across the county. The Eighth AAF personnel were ready to serve. It had been different in the Great War. America was slow to recognise the potential of the aeroplane. When American airmen flew in France in 1918 they used French or British aircraft, having no available military planes of their own. General Billy Mitchell, a US commander, faced a court martial for voicing an opinion on the poor provision. He would have approved of the level of involvement of the USAF in the 1940s. Because so many servicemen were in England, the idea of providing them with a friendly and respectable place to relax was immediately popular. Young men, especially those away from their wives and children, were able to play darts and cards or use the library away from the temptations of the fleshpots of Norwich. There were some! Members of the Women's Voluntary Service helped to run the club at St Clement's.

Below: Dating back to the 13th century, St Andrew's Hall was rebuilt on this site in 1428 by Sir Thomas Erpingham. He was a knight who had led a force of archers at the Battle of Agincourt in 1415. One of the city gates to the cathedral bears his name. In Henry VIII's day, it was one of the churches and monasteries that he dissolved in his purge of the established church. Later bought by the city for the princely sum of £233, most of the value being derived from the lead on the roof, it was used as a fair and hall for use by the mayor and his fellows. It continues to be used as a venue for public meetings and exhibitions to-day. Here we see a civic week exhibition. The various emergency and civil defence organisations had their stands and displays. Old enforcers, truncheons and guns mixing with safety aids like the lifebelt and emergency phone gave the display a strange balance. It did not seem to know quite the message it was trying to get across. However, we could just about deduce that the organisations were linked. The coastguard and other services had the common purpose of helping us. They were all involved in civil defence of one form or another. It was important that we heeded the message about not misusing lifebelts. There had been a spate of thefts from the wooden boxes along sea fronts that were their home.

RG Carter - Building on the success of previous generations

Even as a little boy, Robert George Carter, the founder of the RG Carter Group, had few doubts about what he wanted to be when he grew up - he wanted to be a carpenter, like his grandfather. And this was the very first of many wise decisions which have resulted in the R G Carter Group becoming the successful, well-respected company that it is today.

Robert George Carter spent his childhood with his widowed mother and her parents at Drayton. Young George, as he elected to be called (George was his grandfather's name) left school at fourteen and became a carpenter's apprentice, practising his new skills with the tools he had inherited from his grandfather. After completing his apprenticeship he tried life in London but decided it was not for him. So he returned home and joined a long queue for work outside Youngs, one of Norwich's best-known building firms. One after another the men in front of him were turned away, but when George reached the front of the queue John Youngs offered him a job on the spot. Clearly, even at that early age, he stood out from the crowd.

For the next few years he went from project to project and was involved in a number of grand schemes, such as rebuilding the stable block at Ditchingham Hall and constructing a new wing at Blofield Hall, where he worked with experienced craftsmen who displayed the high levels of skill and craftsmanship that were to become so important to George. In 1914 George Carter joined up and served in France with the 126th Field Company of the Royal Engineers. He was lucky to survive the war. He was wounded twice, and it was feared that he had lost his sight during one gas attack; fortunately this proved not to be the case, but his health was permanently affected. His bravery earned him the Military Medal and the Croix de Guerre. Having refused a commission early in the war, he left the army as Sergeant, and within three days of being demobbed had found himself a job with the London building firm Scott and Middleton, working on the site of Caley's chocolate factory at Chapel Field, Norwich. George's ability quickly earned him promotion to foreman and then to general foreman. Like most builders he did a few private jobs in his spare time, and a lady named Mrs Raikes asked him to fit new windows; by the time the windows were fitted George had fallen in love with Mrs Raike's cook Florence Rolfe, a quiet, gentle woman, daughter of a farmworker from Diss. The young couple were married in 1921. That same year Scott and Middleton's work at Caley's was complete and they asked George to go to Newark where they were to build a bridge, but George wished to stay with his new bride in Norfolk, so as an ambitious young man he decided to leave and concentrate on building up his own business.

From the outset, the whole family was involved in the venture; his uncles helped him financially, Florence acted as secretary, bookkeeper and wages clerk and her brother Ted drove the horse and trolley, later progressing to the firm's first motor lorry. George worked night and day to get his business up and running. He began by building cottages at the Stanninghall Tuberculosis Colony, followed by private houses including some semi-detached properties at Rail

Above left: *RG Carter, founder of the company.*
Below: *Craftsmen in the 1930s with RE Carter as a boy in the centre.*

View, Drayton, one of which became the home of George and Florence, their son Robert Edward, born on 2 December 1922 and daughters Betty, Mary and Ruth.

In 1922 R G Carter carried out his first job for Bullard's, converting buildings at the Anchor Brewery into garages as the brewery moved from horse-drawn vehicles to motor lorries. Ernest Bullard was more than satisfied with his work, and this was the beginning of a relationship which lasted until Bullard's was taken over by Watney's in 1963, with George Carter being invited to build several new pubs as well as undertake renovations and maintenance on others. George also built up a close relationship with another important Norwich brewer, Morgan's Brewery Co Ltd. Among the many pubs built, extended and maintained by the firm for both breweries were the 'White Hart' and the 'Bush Inn' at Costessey, the 'Red Lion' at Drayton, the 'Sceptre' at Great Yarmouth and the 'Bricklayers' Arms' at Bull Close, Norwich.

During the 20s and 30s work included a number of village halls and church buildings, such as Sunday school rooms for the churches in Belvoir Street and Dereham Road, churches for the Christian Scientists and for the Christian Spiritualists, and refurbishment of St Alban's Church at Lakenham; public buildings, such as the Eye, Ear, Nose & Throat block at the Norfolk & Norwich Hospital, the David Rice Hospital in Drayton and the Maternity wing at the Norfolk & Norwich; and, in the late 30s, school contracts such as Norwich Grammar School and Diss secondary school.

> *During the 1920s and 30s work included a number of village halls and church buildings*

The firm was also gaining a reputation for industrial and commercial work, while housing covered everything from estates for private developers and local authorities to individual architect-designed properties. The firm first worked for Norwich City Corporation in 1925, and their first big contract for housing on the Drayton Road estate was followed by houses on the North Earlham estate and flats at Fuller's Hall.

George worked hard, but he always found time for his children, and was a strict but loving father. Where work was concerned, his guiding rule was that a contract had to be completed on time even if it meant working from six in the morning until ten in the evening during the summer months. When a contract was finished he liked to put up hoardings emblazoned with the firm's proud boast, On Time Again! His bricklayers were expected to lay 800-1,000 bricks in an eight hour day, and carpenters had to hang a standard internal door in an hour. George inspected how doors had been hung using an old penny to make sure that the space around the door - the 'penny liberty' - was exact. His workforce learned that he would not tolerate timewasters but would reward hard work. At a time when employment rights were minimal and employers could act in an arbitrary manner, George preferred to keep the same men together and was quite happy to pay for travelling time in order to keep gangs together. His ability to create loyalty among his workforce is

Above: *The original RG Carter offices at Drayton in the 1920s.*

proved by the firm's record of long service and the fact that so many members of the same families were eager to work for R G Carter. All this created a family feeling within the business. George Carter's firm survived the depression of the late 1920s and early 1930s which put many builders out of business, but it was not an easy time.

Some men had to be asked to leave; however, George tried to shed as few workers as possible, and this was appreciated by the men. In 1932 the worst was over and George decided it was time to turn the firm into a limited company, and so R G Carter Ltd began, with a sound reputation based upon quality workmanship, prompt completion and first-rate service. At the heart of the new company lay its expanding workforce, a band of men who were not only talented tradesmen but also completely committed to furthering the firm's reputation. In 1935 the building firm of Herbert Bullen and Sons Ltd became part of R G Carter Ltd. George Carter was by now employing 250 men.

Three years later son Bob, who had been educated at Norwich School, a popular and sociable young man as well as an enthusiastic cricketer, golfer and fisherman, joined the

Top: *The Water Gate, Pulls Ferry, Norwich restored between 1949 and 1950 by the company.*
Above: *This building in Princes Street, Norwich regularly played host to the London Companies during the plague years. It was renovated by the company to retain its Tudor exterior.*
Above left: *Bob Carter.*

firm as an apprentice carpenter. Unfortunately his early career was interrupted, as his father's had been, by the outbreak of war.

Early in the war the firm was involved in the construction of a new naval base at Immingham, as a result of which the business obtained a steady stream of contracts for various Government departments, notably the War Office, the Air Ministry and the Admiralty. One of the more unusual jobs was a contract at Withernsea on Humberside which involved building a fake city, complete with homes and factories, as a decoy to draw German bombers away from the important target of Hull.

Bob Carter returned in 1946, and after completing his apprenticeship he took a correspondence course in quantity surveying. He then started work in the offices at Drayton, which had now moved from Low Road to larger purpose-

built premises in the High Road where R G Carter Ltd remains to this day. By 1950, in order to ensure the continuation of the business, Bob Carter was actively running the company as managing director.

One of the main priorities after the war was the construction of housing, and R G Carter Ltd played a full part in this, building 4,000 houses between 1945-60, principally for local authorities. One foreman was awarded the British Empire Medal for his contribution to the public housing programme.

The company also constructed a number of school and college buildings in and around the city; the new north wing added to Norwich City College & School of Art in Ipswich Road between 1951-3 was the largest building put up in the city since the end of the war. Norwich Training College, a teacher training institution in College Road, destroyed by bombs in 1942, took out a lease on the 19th century Keswick Hall and contracted the company to carry out alterations, following this up a year later with a further contract to build a new east wing. This was opened in April 1951 by the Queen, with George Carter in attendance.

Many important city landmarks which had been destroyed or allowed to fall into decay during the war were restored by the company, and their construction of the Colman Galleries at Norwich Castle, which were opened by Princess Elizabeth in June 1951 marked the emergence of the city from the gloom of the immediate post-war years.

In the early 50s under Bob Carter's leadership, the company exhibited a greater maturity and professionalism and business began to boom. By the mid-1950s, R G Carter had

Left: *A photograph of the founder, Mr RGW Carter being hoisted by Tower Crane to the roof level of the Norwich Union Island site - east tower 1960-61.*
Below: *The structural steel frame for Tower Block 1 above existing shops in the St Stephens Street redevelopment c1970.*

become the largest building firm in Norfolk. Subsidiaries included Bullen's, Fishers, Blackburn's and Drayton Stone Pits; 850 men were employed at Drayton, and 2,000 throughout the Group. Prestigious clients included Norwich Union, for whom the firm first constructed a block of offices and shops in Surrey Street, followed two years later by new offices at 19 Upper King Street. Norwich Union then announced major plans to redevelop the 'island site' bounded by Surrey Street, Westlegate and All Saints Green, the intention being to re-house 2,000 office staff in a new L-shaped block. Before work on that project began, Norwich Union showed its confidence in the company by appointing them as main contractors for an office block at the lower end of Surrey Street. The company completed this three months ahead of schedule in February 1957. In 1958 the multi-million pound contract for the 190,000 square feet, ten-storey office block at All Saints Green for Norwich Union became the firm's second contract in excess of a million pounds; the first had been won the previous year for a new factory in King's Lynn for Campbell's Soups, where the successful execution of the original contract led to more work on the site, and in 1960 the company set up a branch office in King's Lynn.

George Carter died suddenly at his home, Drayton House, in Drayton on 30 September 1966 at the age of 74. The funeral was held at Drayton parish church on 4 October, and in spite of the rain hundreds of people lined the route from the village centre to the church to mourn the loss of a great man. Bob Carter now succeeded his father as chairman. By this time the Group of companies covered an area of 500 square miles and employed 2,500 men. Bob was described as a

perfect gentleman. Although not enjoying the best of health, he had a supreme sense of duty and a determination to uphold standards. As managing director, he had possessed the foresight and vision which had driven the business forward for a decade, allowing it to execute contracts larger and more complex than any it had previously handled and eventually to expand not only into a wider geographical area but also into other activities related to construction.

Under Bob Carter's chairmanship, the Group grew rapidly. Between 1966 and the Group's golden anniversary in 1971, turnover doubled to £15.3 million and the workforce rose to 3,000. Since the Group was carrying out more and more multi-million pound contracts, Bob Carter realised that much more emphasis had to be placed upon financial monitoring. In particular, he recognised that surveying was becoming increasingly important in this context.

One of Bob Carter's ambitions was to initiate a more formal scheme of training within the Group which would provide greater opportunities for more people. He believed that better training would increase efficiency which in itself would create growth, and would also stimulate individual effort by enhancing the prospects of promotion. He introduced a training scheme at Drayton to improve the standard of apprentices; bricklaying was the first trade to become part of the scheme and young brick-layers spent three months on site, training with a general foreman. In October 1969 the Group Training Centre was

Above: *An aerial picture of central Norwich which shows six Carter Group projects being carried out simultaneously.*

opened at the premises in Low Road, Drayton, where the Group had started life in 1921 and remained in existence until August 1976 when it was superseded by the new CITB training centre in Norwich.

In 1967 the company acquired the old-established Norwich firm of John Youngs Ltd, where George Carter was first offered work by John Youngs. This company possessed a distinctive identity and valuable reputation and was run in parallel with R G Carter. Other acquisitions followed as the Group expanded throughout East Anglia. Norwich landmarks completed during this period include: the construction of the Anglia Square development at Magdalen Street which included a shopping centre with cinema as well as an office block for Her Majesty's Stationery Office, the County Hall which was opened by the Queen in 1968 with Bob Carter in attendance, the Hotels Nelson and Norwich built in 1969 and 1971 respectively for Property Partnerships PLC, an eleven storey hospital block built between 1971 and 1974, the first major repairs for more than 500 years to the roof over the North and South aisles of Norwich Cathedral using English oak in 1973, renovation work at Dragon Hall, various multi-storey car parks and numerous office blocks including St Crispins. R G Carter Ltd and its associates also won a design competition organised by Norwich City Council for the redevelopment of the former Bally shoe factory site in Princes Street. The imaginative £500,000 scheme provided for 27 houses and flats with shops and offices. At the same time, a second similar joint venture was agreed for the development of Colegate by building 39 large houses through two joint companies, Colegate Investments Ltd and Colegate Developments Ltd.

The over-rapid growth of the King's Lynn company and its satellites in Grimsby and Hull was causing some difficulties within the Group. Managers locally were pushing for speedy expansion and were not allowing business to develop gradually by establishing a reputation based on smaller contracts. Instead it was based upon large contracts, employing people whose values differed from those on which the Group had been founded and had prospered. Meanwhile, Bob Carter's illness became so acute that he was advised that his only chance of recovery lay in heart surgery. Sadly, he failed to recover from the operation. He died on 21 October 1974 aged 51, leaving a widow, Mary, and four children: sons Robert George, named after his grandfather, John, and daughters Jane and Louise. At his funeral service at St Margaret's in Drayton, the Bishop of Lynn, the Right Reverend Aubrey Aitkin, a family friend, described him as 'a man of Norwich and Norfolk'. More than 2,500 people attended his memorial service in Norwich Cathedral a few days later.

Bob's premature death was devastating not only for his family but also for the R G Carter Group. His elder son, Robert, was now, at an early age, thrust into a very senior role as vice-chairman and joint managing director. While the business was sound, its rapid expansion, combined with a number of loss-making contracts, had left it seriously short of cash. But the Group had tremendous assets in the experience and expertise of its management and also in the loyalty of long-standing clients.

Robert Carter married Charlotte Miller, the daughter of a notable Norfolk architect, on 2 May 1981, and exactly a year later their first child was born, named Robert Edward, after his grandfather, followed by Sophie, James and Camilla. Robert took over as Group chairman that same year as well as running R G Carter Ltd at Drayton as general manager between 1980-2. In his view, the Group's greatest strengths were its building expertise, skilled workforce and expanding reputation. In the increasingly competitive business environment of the recession, Robert Carter was determined to give the Group a commercial edge and make it show a profit in every sphere of activity. Areas like Hull and Wakefield were too far away to be

Below: *Apprentice bricklayers under training.*

properly controlled, and the Group's traditional approach was unsuited to the more aggressive and volatile construction environment further North. Within two years the depth of the recession had forced the closure of the Wakefield and Hull offices. However, the Group's traditional strengths meant it was able to come out of the recession in a stronger position. After these experiences he decided that before any further expansion of the Group took place he would have to be completely convinced of the reasons for it. Having taken the firm back to its roots, further expansion was now possible. The first new office was opened in Peterborough in January 1983, and Peterborough's development was a typical example of how the Group expanded from the 1980s onwards, with steady, progressive, organic growth, rather than growth by acquisition, as the key.

When work began on Colman's new packed goods store at Carrow in 1976, R G Carter Ltd celebrated an association with Colman's stretching back 25 years. In 1979, the company gained a three-year multi-million pound contract from another long-standing client, Anglia Television, for the conversion of the former Post Office building in Norwich into a studio and offices linked to the existing premises completed by the firm ten years previously. At the University of East Anglia, the Group built the Sainsbury Centre for the Visual Arts to house Sir Robert and Lady Sainsbury's art collection. Described as a building with 'panache' in the Architectural Review, it was opened in April 1978 to widespread acclaim from the national press and television, and won prestigious awards including the Royal Institute of British Architects (RIBA) Eastern Region Award and the Special Finniston Award for Structural Design.

In the early 1980s, the Group embarked on a series of major prison contracts; the huge contract for Wayland prison, near Watton, was the largest contract the Group had ever handled. In 1979 the firm built the River End spectator stand for Norwich City Football Club. Then, on 25 October 1984, the main stand at Carrow Road was destroyed by fire

and the company was invited to build a new stand. Two Design & Build schemes were submitted and a contract was signed on 6 November 1985. The new stand, named the 'City Stand' was opened by the Duchess of Kent on 14 February 1987. Five years later, in 1992, the firm completed a third stand for the football club, the Barclay Stand, and this was followed by two further corner in-fill stands linking together all the new structures constructed by the company. In the summer of 1985 the company began refurbishing the Royal Arcade, built by John Youngs nearly a century earlier; this was completed in 1990.

In 1987, the company won the contract to build the new terminal building at Norwich airport, opened on 25 July 1988 by the Queen Mother. Also in 1987 the firm built the Norwich Sport Village, which involved a unique form of undulating freestanding concrete shell structures covering the sports areas. At the same location the firm built the multi-million pound Aquapark complex in 1990. The company was also responsible in 1991 for the major refurbishment of Norwich's Theatre Royal, a contract lasting 44 weeks which was funded largely by business and public donations.

Major projects since then have included a large number of superstores and shopping centres, including Budgen's at Sprowston, International Stores at Watton, the Britten Centre shopping complex in Lowestoft and a new 6,400 metre superstore in Queen's Road, Norwich, for Sainsbury's. For Tesco in 1990-1, the company constructed a 5,100 square metre store at Lowestoft, followed by a major refurbishment of a store in the heart of Norwich, close to the Guildhall, and a 5,750 square metre store at Harford Bridges on the outskirts of Norwich in 1996. Among other major clients for whom the firm has carried out work over many years are Norwich Union, the University of East Anglia, Rhone-Poulenc who had taken over May & Baker, and Property Partnerships PLC. Another

Below: *The new Magistrates Court - built for Norfolk County Council c 1985.*

important client has been the Bernard Matthews organisation, which has used the company repeatedly for new buildings. In 1987, for example, the firm completed Bernard Matthews' new processing plant at Great Witchingham. Business parks were a feature of the late 1980s, and one of the first in the area was the Norwich Business Park at Whiting Road for one of the firm's long-standing clients, Frenbury Properties. In 1993, the company was appointed to carry out the main infrastructure works required at the St Andrew's Business Park at Thorpe, developed to take advantage of the proximity of the new A47 southern bypass. On this site, the firm also won through competition a contract to build both the 6,500 square metre office building occupied by the Central Computer and Telecommunication Agency and the Eastern Counties Newspapers Print Centre. In 1994 the company became directly involved as landowners in the development of Longwater Business Park adjacent to the western section of the A47 bypass and in 1997 constructed a 5,570 square metre store for Sainsbury's in just 26 weeks.

In April 1999 it was announced that the company had been awarded the £22 million main contract to build the new Millennium Library in Norwich, a project that will be of great interest to everyone and establish another important landmark in this fine city.

In the summer of 1996, the firm celebrated its 75th anniversary at The Lowlands in Drayton. Many old friends, clients and staff were present to mark the occasion, as were some 300 pensioners, each of whom had achieved over 25 years of service.

The scope of work undertaken by the R G Carter Group today remains as wide and varied as ever, embracing small works, maintenance and facilities management as well as major construction projects. Since 1982, under the chairmanship of Robert Carter, the Group has enjoyed the most successful period in its history. A crucial element in this success is the whole culture of the Group as a family business which embraces everyone from the most junior apprentice to the most senior director and provides a strong element of security and stability for employees. Also, Robert Carter's firm belief in the continuous recruitment and training of apprentices - something which has always been maintained no matter how difficult things have been - has enabled the Group to sustain its traditional policy of internal promotion, which not only plays a key role in keeping the skilled and experienced workforce together but also helps the personal and family ethos of the Carter Group to be maintained. Thus, the firm established over 75 years ago by Robert Carter's grandfather, is still building for the future.

*Top: An aerial view of Norwich City Football Club stadium showing the three new stands built by the company between 1979 and 1991. **Above left:** The Chairman and some of the original directors (from left to right: Geoffrey Furness, Billy Hunter, Stanley Tuddenham, Robert Carter, Ernie George, Stanley Daynes and Alan Brookes).*

Changing city

It never rains but it pours in Norwich. The uneven surface of the car park cum bombsite is a muddy place to tramp across to get your car. Nicely cleaned shoes this morning will be covered in that dirty, grey mud and concrete dust that we had to negotiate to rescue our motors. The single-decker bus has just come away from Orford Place, splashing pedestrians with rainwater as it ploughed through the puddles. The Bell Hotel holds a good position, able to overlook Red Lion Street, Castle Meadow, Farmers Ave and Timberhill. It is little wonder that it was once an important coaching inn, standing so handily at the meeting place of so many roads.

The square lines of Norwich Castle stand behind it. Some of its original Norman features can still be traced. The Royal Liver Building was offering assistance with house purchase and life and endowment insurance. A better way to escape from the misery of the rain was to have a flutter on the pools with Littlewoods, being advertised on the Corporation double-decker buses. It is the National Lottery these days, but in the 1950s the thought of the untold riches of £75,000 for forecasting eight draws was the flight of fancy we all had. As one famous winner later remarked, it would be an opportunity to 'spend, spend, spend'.

Above: What a mess the war had made. Drinkers in the Bell, the light coloured building towards the top of the picture, could look down towards those supping Bullard's beers and ales in the Orford Arms on Red Lion Street. They would have been of one mind. It was going to take some time before the unsafe buildings were demolished and the rubble cleared. Then the rebirth of the area could take place. In those first few years after the war life had to go on as best it could. Ration coupons were jealously hoarded until there were sufficient to 'size up your taste in fashion' with the fine furnishings on offer next to the Bell Hotel. The insurance loss adjustors in the Burlington Buildings to the left were kept busy handling the heavy volume of claims from those whose belongings had been lost and homes shattered by the onslaught from the skies. The Cricketers', next to the Anchor Buildings on the right, was another place of refuge for those wanting to drown their sorrows. At least the bombsite created a large park for drivers who had no need to worry about finding

somewhere to leave their cars. Curl's department store took advantage of the open space to erect a large hoarding advertising its Westlegate outlet. Visit the Alexon size-right shop for coats, suits and skirts to fit all figures, was its boast. It was all scant consolation for what we had lost.

Top: The grand red brick of the old Agricultural Hall stands as a monument to the blending of old and new. In later years we have come used to seeing Nicholas Parsons walk into the building for 'Live from Norwich, it's the Sale of the Century'. It had become part of the Anglia TV studios. Happily, the old facade was kept. There may be a wonderland of technology within, but old Norwich has been kept on the outside. The cross-roads is known as the Agricultural Hall Plain. The Prince of Wales, later Edward VII, opened the building, in 1882. In his honour, the street at which head it stands was called Prince of Wales Road, leading down and across the river to Thorp Road. Norwich is lucky to have been able to keep many of its fine period buildings. The developers and mad planners have not run riot here as in other British cities. Also on the Plain you can see the similar brickwork of the Royal, that was considered to be the city's finest hotel. The Crown bank, which was later the Post Office, is alongside the Hall. As befits the grandeur of the buildings, it was to the Hall that George Gilbert brought his famous Royal Cinematographe (note the sophistication of the last 'e') in 1897. It showed animated photographs, presenting with 'marvellous accuracy scenes of everyday life'. These scenes included a boat at Yarmouth, the Prince of Wales at Marlborough House and a boxing kangaroo! Some everyday scenes, you might think, but a marvel of their age. How fitting that pictures are still coming from here.

A glance at the 1940s

HOT OFF THE PRESS

At the end of World War II in 1945 the Allies had their first sight of the unspeakable horrors of the Nazi extermination camps they had only heard of until then. In January, 4,000 emaciated prisoners more dead than alive were liberated by the Russians from Auschwitz in Poland, where three million people, most of them Jews, were murdered. The following year 23 prominent Nazis faced justice at Nuremberg; 12 of them were sentenced to death for crimes against humanity.

THE WORLD AT LARGE

The desert area of Alamogordo in New Mexico was the scene of the first atomic bomb detonation on July 16, 1945. With an explosive power equal to more than 15,000 tons of TNT, the flash could be seen 180 miles away. President Truman judged that the bomb could secure victory over Japan with far less loss of US lives than a conventional invasion, and on 6th August the first of the new weapons was dropped on Hiroshima. Around 80,000 people died.

ROYAL WATCH

By the end of World War II, the 19-year-old Princess Elizabeth and her distant cousin Lieutenant Philip Mountbatten RN were already in love. The King and Queen approved of Elizabeth's choice of husband, though they realised that she was rather young and had not mixed with many other young men. The engagement announcement was postponed until the Princess had spent four months on tour in Africa. The couple's wedding on 20th November 1947 was a glittering occasion - the first royal pageantry since before the war.

Standing on the castle ramparts and gazing west across the city, the Catholic cathedral of St John's appears in the distance. To the left is the distinctive sight of the church of St Peter Mancroft. However, the centre of local government, the City Hall, dominates the scene. Its clean Scandinavian lines were designed by CH James and SR Pierce. There had been much interest in Egyptian styles in the years leading up to the final design. Features of an Egyptian

flavour can be found on the Hall. Public imagination had been fired by the discoveries of Carter and Caernarvon in the 1920s. Tutankhamen's tomb and the curses and mysteries surrounding it had been a fascination brought to the nation by the growing popularity of the cinema newsreel. The rearing Abyssinian lions at the front guard the entrance steps to its fine bronze doors and the reliefs of industry past and present on its facade. Replacing the old municipal buildings, King

George VI presided at its official opening in 1938. When it was new its orange colour led it to be nicknamed by locals as the 'marmalade hall'. The imposing clock tower stands out like a beacon and can be seen from most parts of the city. It's often a good directional guide for visitors who lose a sense of direction in Norwich's narrow streets. One look upward to the tower and the position of the city centre can be judged. No need for a compass when you have that aid.

Looking across Chapelfield Street and up St Giles Street on the left, the city stretches eastwards towards Kett's Hill and Gas Hill on the far side. The shop awnings have been pulled down to keep the sun from fading and perishing the goods. Within the city life is just beginning, this day over 30 years ago. Rising out above the skyline are the steeples and spires of some of Norwich's many churches and cathedrals. In mediaeval times there were 57 churches. Many of them were perpendicular in style and built of local flint. Even now, 31 still exist. Flanked by the wider streets we can see here are the narrower alleyways and byways that mark the character of the city centre. It was lucky that many of these older and more historic areas avoided the carnage of the second world war blitz. The high rise flats and multi-storey office buildings don't mar the landscape. Without the cars in the picture, this could be a scene from any period of the 20th century. Around every corner of every little street is a sight waiting to surprise you. A shop you hadn't noticed before, down a side passage you hadn't explored until now, was waiting to be discovered. Norwich is a city in an orchard, surrounded as it is with delightful countryside. At the time we are looking at it, Norwich has been able to balance being a city of many strands. As the busy centre of an agricultural region it has both valued and preserved its past. At the same time, it is modern and forward looking to what the third millennium will bring.

Above: The YMCA was established on Bethel Street in 1854. The entrance to the hostel is made from St Giles Street, once the city's medical quarter. Behind it is the alleyway of Rigby's Court. The association's training centre has been around the corner since 1986. Alongside the hostel entrance is in inscription announcing that here is a lecture hall and gymnasium. To underpin the caring side of St Giles Street, the Norwich Citadel Corps of the Salvation Army, with its blood and fire logo, occupies another of the buildings nearby. A roller skating rink once stood there. The YMCA had begun in London, in 1844. The draper, George Williams, had started a club for the improvement of the spiritual condition of young men in the drapery and other trades. The clubs, aimed to promote high standards of Christian character and citizenship training. The growth was rapid. By the early 1850s clubs had appeared in Montreal, Boston and Australia. YMCA programmes include sports and physical education, camp-

ing, counselling, formal and informal education. It has clung to its belief in cherishing a non-political and non-sectarian Christian ethic. Sadly, the image was a bit tarnished by the 1978 hit record by a group called Village People. This camp outfit, dressed in various silly costumes, sang about the virtues of the YMCA, but their efforts provoked amusement rather than respect.

Top: If you suffer from vertigo, look away now. Quite how the photographer hung onto his hat is not revealed, but his position must have been very precarious. No doubt the good Lord was taking care, because the scene is viewed from the Catholic Cathedral of St John's. From here roads lead out behind the cameraman along Earlham Road and Unthank Road. On this latter street is the old rectory of St John's Maddermarket church, a source of religious solace for players and actors. Mr John Unthank sold the rectory to the church in 1864. Unthank is a name which is Scandinavian in origin and dates back to a time when the Vikings were pillaging and doing whatever else it was that Vikings did. The largely perpendicular church of St Giles, just off the top of the picture, dates from around 1420-30. The beautiful wisteria surrounding the churchyard makes it a most picturesque sight so close to the city centre. The tower, at its parapet that goes back to 1737 stands 113 ft and is the highest in the city. The present chancel appeared in 1866 and replaced one that had been lost in 1581. St Giles Street has always been an important one. Sweep away from the main Chapelfield Rd and, from St Giles Gate, you can race straight down to City Hall and Market Place.

Theatre Street, as you might guess, has been home to some of Norwich's artistic and dramatic folk. Thomas Ivory built the Assembly House in 1754. It has hosted concerts, exhibitions and meetings. A restaurant was a popular inclusion, giving audiences the opportunity to dine within easy reach of their concert seats. At first it was a large ballroom and tea room for polite society of the 18th and 19th century. During a later life it became a girls' school. Henry Sexton restored it to a more fitting role after World War II. The Theatre Royal dates from the same period, seeing the light of day for the first time in 1758. It has needed to be rebuilt twice since then. In the late 1940s and early 1950s restoring the parts of the city scarred and ruined by the war was begun. On the right Curl's department store is taking shape. It would soon again dominate this corner, inviting us in to browse amongst the variety on offer. Behind Boots, the Haymarket was a favourite cinema until its closure in the mid 50s. These were the days of the Saturday children's matinee. For a tanner you could join the company of the hilarious Three Stooges, ride with Hopalong Cassidy and thrill to the serialised adventures of Flash Gordon. Buster Crabbe, who played the title role, was left in a death-threatening predicament every week. We just had to dig in our pockets once again the following Saturday to see how he escaped, because he always did.

cuts St Giles' Street. The VW Beetle could, very probably, be driving along here to-day. Other than the number plate, there would be little to distinguish it in shape from the successors that would bear the same model name.

Top: Norwich is well blessed with churches. Wherever you look in the city, one tower or another is there to be seen. In the Middle Ages various orders of friars and monks, including Augustinians, Dominicans and Carmelites, made their homes here. Rich merchants supported them and helped with improvements to the churches that were to spring up. Later, Presbyterians, Quakers and Congregationalists settled in different quarters of the city. In the more tolerant days of the 19th century, Catholic churches grew in importance. Standing above most of them on the skyline is the church of St Giles. It has the tallest tower of any of Norwich's parish churches. There was once a beacon with fire burning in the iron basket on top of the tower. The present chancel was built in 1866. The burly man in the foreground could be heading there for a moment's quiet contemplation. It is also possible that he is off for a haircut at the gents' hairdressing saloon on the right. The 1960s were a bit too soon for him to contemplate a unisex salon. The barber's seems to be doubling as a post office, which is a strange thought. He could always pop in to the teashop for a cuppa or a Lyons Maid ice-cream cornet. On the other hand, he could cross over for a fine pint of Bullard's ale.

Above: It is remarkable how well loved the people's car of Nazi Germany came to be by the British public. We are, generally speaking, an easy-going people. Old scores are seldom continued vendetta-style. By 1960 the 'Beetle', with its distinctive curving bonnet, was better known by that single word, rather than as the Volkswagen. Across the road we can see St Giles' Gates. The original gates stood next to a leper house. They were once one of 12 such gates built into the city wall, dating from the 14th century. They gave access to and from the city and were used to collect tolls that helped in the upkeep of city defences. When the rebel Robert Kett led an assault on Norwich in the 16th century, many of the gates were damaged. Although they were repaired, the cost of their maintenance became too much for the Corporation to bear. Most were demolished around 1800. At one time the gates that stood here were called Newport Gates, after the former name of St Giles' Street and Bethel Street. This area is now where the new part of the inner link road

On the move

Above: When, just after midnight, the 16th air raid of the war arrived in the skies above the city, the bombs cut a swathe through Vauxhall Street, off Chapelfield Road. The little businesses and houses along here were badly damaged. Four homes were completely wrecked and hardly any of the others in the vicinity escaped without some effect from the high explosives and incendiaries. It had once been a quiet backwater. Even the advertising on the wooden fence is unobtrusive. The signs are devoted to two good old standbys of British life, jam and tea. Say 'Bon' to Brooke Bond was one message. In later years we would come to enjoy the antics of the chimps that were used to promote the product. They have been with us for donkey's years and are as much loved as the cup of tea they promote. We have always had a soft spot for animals. The Silver Shred and Golden Shred marmalades continue to appear on supermarket shelves. Their tangy lemon and orange flavours make that piece of breakfast toast all the more satisfying. However, the 'perfect jelly preserve' of Robertson's Golliberry has disappeared. There was such a fuss about the Robertson's golly badges we used to collect as children. They were said to stereotype and caricature Afro-Caribbeans. As nippers we did not realise that, the badge was just a little prize, but political correctness held the day and Golliberry was not seen again.

Above right: Barrack Street, with its well known puppet theatre at one end, still keeps some of an older feel to it. As part of the inner ring road around the city, its main use now is to channel traffic in from Thorpe and the Plumsteads. The Esso sign, which meant happy motoring in the TV adverts of May 1972, indicated that here was fuel for your car. Happily trundling away opposite was the milk float, the source of fuel for your offspring. But, alongside the garage, was the fount of

sustenance for the drinker. Various breweries had homes in the city at one time. Names such as Morgan's and Young's, Crawshay and Young's spring to mind. Coleman's came to prominence with the curative powers of its internationally famous Wincarnis tonic wine. Many an old dear pronounced that she needed to have the odd glass, purely for its medicinal purposes. Here was the site of the Steward and Patteson brewery. Walking past any day was a special treat for the nasal passages. The aroma of malt extract, hops, barley and all the ingredients for a good pint hung in the air. If you breathed in often enough as you walked along you felt quite light-headed. Brewing was a particularly important industry in the 19th century. There was a vast number of small independent brewers. In those days many pubs brewed their own beers and ales. Norwich, however, had the smallest number of such pubs in the whole of Britain, relying more on the city's small breweries to supply them. The street is named after the former cavalry barracks, built there in 1791.

Below: Everyone knows the Bell Hotel. It's one of the city landmarks and directional points. Farmers Avenue? Turn right off Red Lion Street, up by the Bell. Castle Mall shopping centre? It's on Castle Meadow, across from the Bell. It's reassuring that important landmarks and buildings such as these have kept their external features much as they were. The character of the city centre pub of yesterday has been preserved. If you want plastic, go somewhere else. The Bell, as it looks now, dates back well into the 18th century. It is one of the few coaching inns to still survive the passage of time. For the younger reader, that doesn't refer to the coach on the pub car park! Before that, there had been a hostelry of some form here in the 15th century. Goodness only knows how many quarts and flagons have been quaffed through the centuries. Enough to fill the Broads, no doubt. It was once called the Blue Bell and has had a chequered career. Many clubs used it as a meeting place. One such was the Tory Hell-Fire Club and the Revolution Club of 1793. In 1754, the preachers, John and Charles Wesley, were attacked by a gang of ruffians and wrote angrily of their experience. The car park was the terminus for local coaches and those going to Yarmouth, so the bus pictured might not be out of place, remembering its ancestors.

A glance at the 1940s

MELODY MAKERS
The songs of radio personalities such as Bing Crosby and Vera Lynn were whistled, sung and hummed everywhere during the 1940s. The 'forces' sweetheart' brought hope to war-torn Britain with 'When the Lights go on Again', while the popular crooner's 'White Christmas' is still played around Christmas time even today.
Who can forget songs like 'People Will Say we're in Love', 'Don't Fence Me In', 'Zip-a-dee-doo-dah', and 'Riders in the Sky'?

INVENTION AND TECHNOLOGY
Inspired by quick-drying printers' ink, in 1945 Hungarian journalist Laszlo Biro developed a ballpoint pen which released viscous ink from its own reservoir as the writer moved the pen across the page. An American inventor was working on a similar idea at the same time, but it was Biro's name that stuck. A few years later Baron Bich developed a low cost version of the pen, and the 'Bic' ballpoint went on sale in France in 1953.

SCIENCE AND DISCOVERY
In 1943 Ukrainian-born biochemist Selman Abraham Waksman made a significant discovery. While studying organisms found in soil he discovered an antibiotic (a name Waksman himself coined) which was later found to be the very first effective treatment for tuberculosis. A major killer for thousands of years, even the writings of the ancient Egyptians contain stories of people suffering from tuberculosis. Waksman's development of streptomycin brought him the 1952 Nobel Prize for Medicine.

Above: Norwich grew from three or four small Saxon settlements, eventually taking its name from one of them, Northwic. Another such hamlet was Westwic. The mechanic seen at work is on the site of that old place as he is working at the Westwick depot. The Norwich Education Committee's van needed an overhaul. Tyres, brakes and bodywork were to be checked before the school meals' driver set off on his rounds. A lot of schools cooked meals in their own kitchens, but this was not always the case. In addition, the smaller, rural village schools had to have meals cooked in the central kitchens and then have them ferried out. What joys would come across the serving hatch in those early post-war days. The welfare state had been born and, under the 1944 Education Act, every child at school had the right to receive a full meal at lunchtime. For the more needy it might be the only hot meal of the day. At 12 o'clock we would troop off to the dining hall. Boiled cabbage that had been stewing since first thing this morning, a lump of meat in its congealed fat and some mash with black bits in was just the nourishing fare for a growing nine year old. Best of all there was lumpy semolina or sago to follow. The dinner ladies and teachers then told you to eat it all up, and no talking. How could you with your mouth bunged up with rice pudding skin?

Right: Young's, Crawshay and Young's, providing the beer on the right of the view of Red Lion Street, was just one of many local brewers in and around the city. Many of these smaller firms were swallowed up by the giant breweries in the latter half of the 20th century. As this happened, the Campaign for Real Ale (CAMRA) was born. Promoting the benefits of the taste of hand drawn pints and proper bits settling to the bottom of the glass, these campaigners had some success in keeping open and, even, relaunching some of the smaller and homelier brewers. That was not in the minds of the people hurrying along the pavement. Beside them was the constant reminder of what the Luftwaffe had brought to the city in the early 40s. The rubble of fine buildings, the cleared bombsites and the weeds pushing through where once shops and offices stood brought back the terror and fear of those times all too vividly. The howl of the bomb as it fell through the sky and the awful momentary silence before it detonated was a nightmare that for some would be a long time in leaving. On a lighter note, take a careful look at the double row of cars parked in the lower centre. How are those to the right going to get out? Is this a case of totally thoughtless parking on the part of those behind? On the other hand, maybe they are all friends and are going to leave work or finish their shopping at exactly the same time. It is to be hoped that this was so or there might be one or two temperaments being tested.

The military airfield on the outskirts of Norwich can trace its origins back over half a century, to early 1939. Horsham St Faith was designated a 'Light Bomber Station', and was of simple construction, initially with a grass landing area, five rudimentary hangars and a handful of supporting buildings. The second world war began before construction work was completed. By 1940 fighter squadrons were using the airfield as a forward base from which they would patrol the

vital shipping lanes of the North Sea. This photograph dates from March 1953, some 14 years after the airfield at Horsham St Faith became operational. The Commander-in-Chief of Fighter Command, Air Marshall Sir Basil Embry, can be seen on the dais as members of 74 squadron proudly march past. Notice the tiger skin on the dais - 74th Squadron's mascot at the time, and not something we would expect to see in more conservation-minded days.

Above: There were emotional scenes at the end of the second world war when the majority of American service personnel returned home. This delightful photograph depicts one such occasion, as villagers from Horsham St Faith wave hats and hankies at a departing Liberator, about to make the arduous journey across the Atlantic to the USA. The designation of Horsham St Faith as an American Air Force Station took place in September 1942. The base remained under American control until May 1945. Aircraft left with up to 20 men on board. Despite their relatively short stint at Horsham St Faith, the brave men flew on 240 sorties which delivered a total of over 13000 tons of bombs behind enemy lines. During the war a total of 65 USAF planes failed to return to the airfield at Horsham St Faith.

Below: 'It is dangerous to open this door when the aircraft is moving,' proclaims the sign on this Handley Page aircraft. It seems amusing to the modern eye, but the notice reminds us of just how 'new' the world of air travel was in 1926 when the photograph was taken. For the princely sum of 6d local people could inspect the interior of the sturdy Handley Page - dreaming perhaps of the possibility of one day travelling by air to some far-away destination. The scene was captured at Mousehold Aerodrome.

Bottom: Norwich was once a significant player in the world of aircraft manufacturing. Boulton and Paul was established in 1797 by William Moore, an ironmonger in Crocker Lane. Eventually the company grew and developed interests in a wide range of manufacturing activities - one being the construction of aeroplanes during the first world war. This photograph was taken in 1918. Sopwith Camels were build initially at the Rose Lane works, but eventually more capacity was needed and new premises were acquired which became the Riverside Works. During the Great War up to 43 aircraft per week were constructed here - a significant achievement by the local workforce of 2000. In all, well over 2000 of the precious machines were built in Norwich - for service with the Royal Flying Corps, the Royal Naval Air Service, and the Belgian, Greek and American airforces.

The provision market is in full swing. In front of the massive presence of the church of St Peter Mancroft is the Sir Garnet Wolseley Hotel. Born in Dublin, Wolseley was a famous field marshal during Victoria's reign. He was instrumental in modernising the British army. Seeing active service throughout the world, particularly in Canada and Africa, he was responsible for seizing the Suez Canal and attempting to rescue General Gordon from the siege of Khartoum. Having a drink here is a good thought when you've finished battling for bargains in the market. Seven centuries ago the market stretched from Guildhall Hill almost to St Stephen's Church. There was a good sense of order, even so. Places were set aside for the sale of meat, fish, vegetables, cloth,

shoes etc and a small spot designated for the use of those who had brought in produce from their small-holdings out in the countryside. As overcrowding became more of a problem, the livestock market was moved to below the castle mound in 1738. In 1960 it moved on to Harford Bridge. Before the coming of City Hall, the market encouraged an even greater variety of activities than you get today. The noise of the street traders shouting the virtue of their wares, the jangling of the barrel organ grinder, the dancing bears, Punch and Judy shows, dentists pulling teeth and quack doctors selling patent medicines made it a mad and vibrant place. The market of the 1990s has its moments, though, as you listen to the humour of the stallholder trying to part you from your money.

Shopping spree

Below: Passing Curls, coming away from Hardy's Furnishing Centre and Evans' Outsize shop, once the height of fashion and regarded as a good example of the neat design of the British motor manufacturer, this saloon looks a world away from the low-slung hatchbacks of 1999. This venerable gentleman of the road, if still alive, would be about 50 by now. What about the pedestrians waiting for it to pass? Do they look as old-fashioned to the modern generation? St Stephen's Plain, or crossroads to those unfamiliar with the term, was once known as Bunting's Corner. This name was lost in World War II when the Bunting's store burnt down. It was common practice in the first half of the 20th century to refer to crossroads and major junctions with the name of an important or well-known building that stood there. If it was a shop or store, so much the better for the owners. It was free advertising. St Stephen's Street, leading to it, was once a street of many inns and taverns. They bore unusual and distinctive names, such as the Unicorn and Loyalty. In late Victorian times the plain was a busy tram crossing. The old tramlines criss-crossed the street and it was important that you kept your wits about you as a tram could easily catch you unawares as it swung round the corner as you were trying to cross. The plain and its surrounds were badly bomb damaged in the last war. Major reconstruction of the buildings and nearby roads took place. The city's first multi-storey car park, a mixed blessing, was built on St Stephen's Street.

After the war, Norwich embarked on remodelling some of its streets. Partly, this was down to the after effects of bomb damage. But, the town planners had further thoughts for the shopper. Cars were banned from a number of the main shopping areas. Note the law-abiding souls pushing their bikes. Quite right, too. This helped make it a more pleasant experience as you could amble happily and safely along the shop fronts. The first street to become pedestrians only was London Street. It was paved in 1965. The Royal Mail van was allowed, being on official bank delivery business. In this picture we look along its elegance in October 1965. At the turn of the millennium, classy clothes shops such as Jaeger, Gap, Laura Ashley and Edinburgh Wool have outlets here. At one end is the large department store of Jarrold's and at the other we come to a financial and legal quarter. Several solicitors' offices and banks have premises along London Street. One of the most impressive buildings is that of the National Provincial Bank. With its imposing 1924 bell tower, it has an almost church-like feel to its architecture. Opie Street was once known as Devil's Alley because of the 18th century sedan chair trade that plied from here. It was named in honour of Amelia and John Opie. She was a novelist of local renown and he was a court portrait painter. Staunch Quakers, they worshipped at the Octagon Chapel on Colegate.

we had lost shillings and pence as well as the personal touch of the shopkeeper. Ask your nipper to-day, 'Where do get bananas come from?' and you will be told, 'Tesco's, and don't forget your club card.'

Top: Gentleman's Walk, running from the corner of London Street to the Haymarket, has clothes and shoe shops, bookshops and jewellers. Go along it and you will see around there Burton's, Next, Wallis, H Samuel, Kay and other familiar names. In the early 1960s it was very similar. The names may change, but their function is little altered. True-Form (sometimes Tru-form) sold the shoes and John Lewis the clothes. Lambert's did a natty line in silk cravats and woollen ties. You get fully kitted out from top to toe by just walking a few yards. That was in the days of imperial measures. You'd have to say a few metres, now. The Walk, as it is known locally, is now pedestrianised, forming part of that inner circle of walkways and paved streets off to the east of Market Place. In its early days the Walk was known as Nether or Lower Way. It became a major place for city people to promenade. That would be called strutting your stuff, to those of you of more tender years. In Regency times it was the place to be seen, as the elegant men about town took the air. So, the name, Gentleman's Walk, was born. The remodelling of Market Place and the building of City Hall, added to the danger of being caught outside in wartime, ended the practice. It was no longer quite the place to be and styles had changed, along with so much else, after those dark days of 1939-45.

Above: In between St Giles Street and London Street, at this corner of Market Place, is the old Gaol Hill. Walk out of the lovely period feel of the Guildhall and there's Tesco's straight in your face. It comes as something of a shock if you weren't expecting it. Centuries of tradition, history and architecture are wiped away with a single glance at those wire baskets and trolleys that have plenty of legroom for your toddler, but little for your bottles. The supermarket was still something of a novelty to these 1967 shoppers. It was a bit like cheating. To be a proper shopper you should go to the right shop for meat, the correct one for bread, find the one that sold fruit and veg and so on. Children were taught that the grocer sold tea and packets of sugar. Flowers came from the florist. To go and get it all from under one roof you were letting down the sisterhood of housewives. As the little specialist food shops felt the pinch and closed, even those of us who hadn't been seduced by the lower prices gave in to the pull of the supermarket. The liberation of the 60s is looked back on with affection. But, within four years of this picture,

This is the heart of Norwich. Local government has been run from the City Hall since just before World War II, but the link with bygone days is seen in the Guildhall to the right. Norwich was granted city status as far back as 1194. During the Middle Ages it grew in size and wealth, being once second only to London in its importance. The charter of 1404 allowed the city to appoint a mayor, two sheriffs and aldermen to run the business and affairs of Norwich. The Guildhall could now be built. Work began in 1407 on the site of what had been a Norman toll house. Conscripted and forced labour was used to speed up the building. It became the seat of local government until the opening of City Hall. In all that time there must have been 529 successive mayors. Will the present seat of government be able to boast the same, should it still stand in 2466? The market stalls, packed together on

Market Place, are a focal point for shoppers and visitors to the city. Surrounded by a large agricultural area, for centuries Norwich has been an important market town. The Saxons had their market in Tombland. After the Normans invaded in 1066, the market centre moved here. Small markets and fairs continued to be held in Tombland for several hundred years, but the main centre of open air trading was firmly established here.

A glance at the 1950s

WHAT'S ON?
Television hit Britain in a big way during the 1950s. Older readers will surely remember 'Double Your Money', Dixon of Dock Green and 'Dragnet' (whose characters' names were changed 'to protect the innocent'). Commercial television was introduced on 22nd September 1955, and Gibbs SR toothpaste were drawn out of the hat to become the first advert to be shown. Many believed adverts to be vulgar, however, and audiences were far less than had been hoped for.

GETTING AROUND
The year 1959 saw the development of the world's first practical air-cushion vehicle - better known to us as the hovercraft. The earliest model was only able to travel at slow speeds over very calm water and was unable to carry more than three passengers. The faster and smoother alternative to the sea ferry quickly caught on, and by the 1970s a 170-ton car-carrying hovercraft service had been introduced across the English Channel.

SPORTING CHANCE
The four-minute mile had remained the record since 1945, and had become regarded as virtually unbreakable. On 6th May 1954, however, Oxford University student Roger Bannister literally ran away with the record, accomplishing the seemingly impossible in three minutes 59.4 seconds. Bannister collapsed at the end of his last amazing lap, even temporarily losing his vision. By the end of the day, however, he had recovered sufficiently to celebrate his achievement in a London night club!

Above: In his candy-striped box, the traffic policeman keeps the traffic moving along Rampant Horse Street. At the top of the picture is St Stephen's Church. It was the last great Norwich church to have been built. The chancel was completed in 1522 and its tower remodelled in 1601. On it are delightful flint and stone roundels, diamonds and window outlines. The last prioress of Campsey is depicted in a small brass that can be found under a trap door in the north aisle. Centre stage, though, belongs to the imposing M & S building, with St Stephen's Street. running away to the left. The great chain inherited the building from Bunting's. No major city or town is complete without its 'Marks and Sparks', as it is affection- ately known. The owner of the St Michael brand name was started as a series of penny bazaars in the north. Michael Marks and Thomas Spencer joined forces in 1894 in the market hall at Wigan, in Lancashire. The stores have become a byword for quality clothing, without being too trendy. White blouses, grey pleated skirts and practical cardigans would see many a Norwich schoolgirl sorted out for the new school year. The business flourished after the war as reliability was guaranteed. From where else could hubby get your undies for that special birthday present? He could hardly risk setting foot in a lingerie shop and coming all over embarrassed. While he was there he could get himself some sensible socks. By 1999, however, M & S was seeing falling profits as the tastes of the modern generation demanded a little more excitement and less in the way of steady-Eddie styles.

Above right: Behind here is the Norwich Union building, but, at the moment, it is Bonds that takes centre stage. This unusual store has quite futuristic, sweeping lines to its delightful bowed shape. Built in a time when most architects were looking for square and straight

edges, it shows what can be done with a little thought. The blend with the curve that is All Saints Green makes it seem as if it had been carefully poured from a jelly mould. A branch of the John Lewis chain, it stands looking at the Mecca, these days. Not everything can be perfect in life. Large department stores, rather than a multitude of little boutiques, have always been part of the character of Norwich. There are some of the more modern style in the city, but around here is the home of the 'grand shop'. Just a few yards up the street you can find Marks and Spencer and Debenhams. Today is probably a Sunday, from the state of the pavements. The cars may have brought worshippers into one of the many churches nearby. Not for us, in the late 50s and early 60s, the mixed blessing of Sunday shopping. If there were eight days in a week shops would open every day, if they could, in our modern world. Didn't you just love it when you could have a day of rest? For the churchgoer it was a chance to be at peace with his maker. For the rest, it gave an opportunity to have a lie in and relax.

Below: At one time the Royal Arcade was the yard to the Royal Hotel coaching inn. Coaches would clatter their way out into what is now Market Place, where many other such inns where sited. The place was a source of busy noise, something that continues today. Walking into the arcade for the first time is not unlike entering a time that man forgot. Originally, there were 24 shops and a Conservative club here, on its 247 foot length. The width of 15 feet is modest, but the 29 feet up to the glass roof are a delight. Seen here in September 1968, the out of place strip lighting has been replaced by huge period wrought iron and glass lanterns, suspended above the glazed Doulton tiles which make up the walkway. That they are decorated with the blue of the peacock is a pretty touch. George Skipper, who built in it 1899, would have approved. The whole art nouveau feel is of a different world. Other effects, such as the bow of the windows, the gold lettering on black and the stained glass window with its stylised trees are a credit to the imagination of the designer. He even brought in Italian workmen to give it that authentic touch. The arcade has been described as a fragment of the Arabian Nights being dropped into the city. A century might have passed since its opening, but such shops as Zuckerman's patisserie and delicatessen keep that continental and cosmopolitan flavour.

Bottom: 'I may be little and I'm stuck in this push chair, but who do you think you are pointing that camera at me? I have come out with my dad for a quiet morning's shopping and window gazing on the Royal Arcade. It's one of the Saturday treats my dad and I have. We look at the pretty angles and bows of the windows as we come in from the Walk. The polished wooden frames around the shop windows always take my eye. There are some real quality goods to be had along here. It was in this very jeweller's that the old man bought mum's engagement ring, but that was when I wasn't even a twinkle in his eye. I do remember him getting her a smart leather handbag, just further down from here. I think it was her birthday, or at least that's what she said it must have been for him to buy her something. I don't know what she meant by that. Did you know that George Skipper, the man whose idea the Arcade was, also designed buildings for the Norwich Union and built the town hall up the coast at Cromer? We might be going up there to-morrow and catch a crab or two, if the weather perks up. Soon we will be going to have a sit down at the little café that's along here. Dad usually has one of those frothy Italian coffees. He looks as if he's got a moustache when he's finished drinking it. We'll sit outside at one of the tables. Dad says it's like gay Paree. I don't know where that is, but it sounds foreign. Perhaps it's in Suffolk.'

Above: The audio part of the former showroom at Snelling's on Blofield Heath lacks the razzmatazz of the electrical superstore and its cunning spotlit display stands and featured special offers. What it doesn't lack are the memories these machines recall. For the dealer it was a case of little acorns developing into the oak tree the business is to-day. For us nostalgia buffs it will recall a day nearly 40 years ago when we plugged in our large, lumpy reel to reel tape recorder to the radio. David Jacobs was about to play a recording of 'Samantha' and introduce the top twenty hit records. We just had to tape the latest Billy Fury or Neil Sedaka song. The Ferguson made transistors for happy families, we were told. It was true. 'Two-way family favourites' would be coming down the airwaves with Cliff and Jean discussing the weather in Berlin. We could tape some of that, too. What fun was to be had with the dual tracking, dubbing one sound over another. Tune to 208 on the Grundig and Pye radio and there was Barry Alldis beaming in all the way from Luxembourg. The Fidelity and the Dansette were the teenager's pride and joy. Mum and dad had gramophones; we had record players. Our vinyl was different, too. Music was played on 45s, not those old 78s. Roll over Beethoven and tell Tchaikovsky the news.

It is said that Queen Elizabeth I once rode side-saddle down here in the 16th century. She wouldn't have had much joy in 1970. By then, the streets were facing the sort of congestion that would gridlock many a city centre. In one way pedestrians were safer crossing the road than they had ever been. The traffic moved so slowly, if at all, that it was hard to imagine anyone ever being knocked down. At least the drivers had time to admire the fine Marks and Spencer building as they waited to move the next few yards along. It is one of the largest of the M & S stores in the country. It is hard to imagine that the empire began with a market stall in

Leeds in the 1890s before opening a store in Wigan in 1931. The Minis in the queue of traffic might have been plucked from the 1969 film, 'The Italian Job'. They won't be doing much in the way of high speed getaways on this day. Approaching the plain at Rampant Horse Street, it is because St Stephen's Street is the main route in from the south that the snarl-up has taken place. The road had been widened in the 1960s, but it had not done enough. On a busy Saturday it took ages to make your way into the centre car parks. The problem did not finish there. There was still the crawl out again at the end of the day.

Above: The Norwich Union building is a good vantage point for seeing across the city. Looking over the roof of Marks and Spencer, spreading before us is the Curl's store, one of the main department stores before and after World War II. The building is prominent today, but is now Debenham's. Behind it is Boots. This part of Norwich has a selection of major department stores, so you do not have far to travel on a shopping spree. The church tower rising above the stores belongs to that of St Peter Mancroft. As it is the largest church in the city it is often mistaken by first time visitors who think it is the Cathedral. It was erected between 1430 and 1455. It owes its origins to the Norman colony that had grown up nearby and had worshipped in the first church on this site. Standing on the southern corner of Market Place, it keeps watch on the activities below and is a constant link with Norwich's heritage. The unusual second name comes from 'magna crofta', Latin for 'great field'. It must have been an even more magnificent sight in mediaeval and Tudor times, sitting amidst a green sward in all its majesty. There is a delightful window on the eastern side of the church that has been there since it was built. An explosion in the 17th century during the English Civil War damaged it. Despite that, it is still a thing of beauty. The spire was added to the great west tower in 1895.

Right: Davey Place runs parallel with the Royal Arcade and along towards the steps up to the castle. Shopping along here has changed little since the early 70s scene we see here. The shops may have changed in name and style, but the pattern of shopping is very similar. That's one of the good things about Norwich. Change for change's sake has never been the watchword. Change if we want to or have to has been the better maxim. Just in case you think that means that Norwich folk are fuddy-duddy or stick in the mud, think again. More to the point, look again. Under the shoppers' feet is a flagged walkway. This is a pedestrianised district. It was so in 1813. Revolutionary in its time, there were eyebrows raised at the thought of banning horses and carriages. However, the people of the Regency period came to accept it, and so it stayed as an example to others. It was the brainchild of Alderman Jonathan Davey. He kept his plans a secret. All that he would tell people was that he intended to put a hole in the king's head. Aware of Norwich's rather colourful past, in terms of revolution and rebellion, the militia was alerted and Davey given a police guard. When Davey bought the King's Head pub and knocked it through to create Davey Place, his joke became clear. Whilst ardent royalists appreciated Davey's rebuilding of the pub, not all understood his sense of humour.

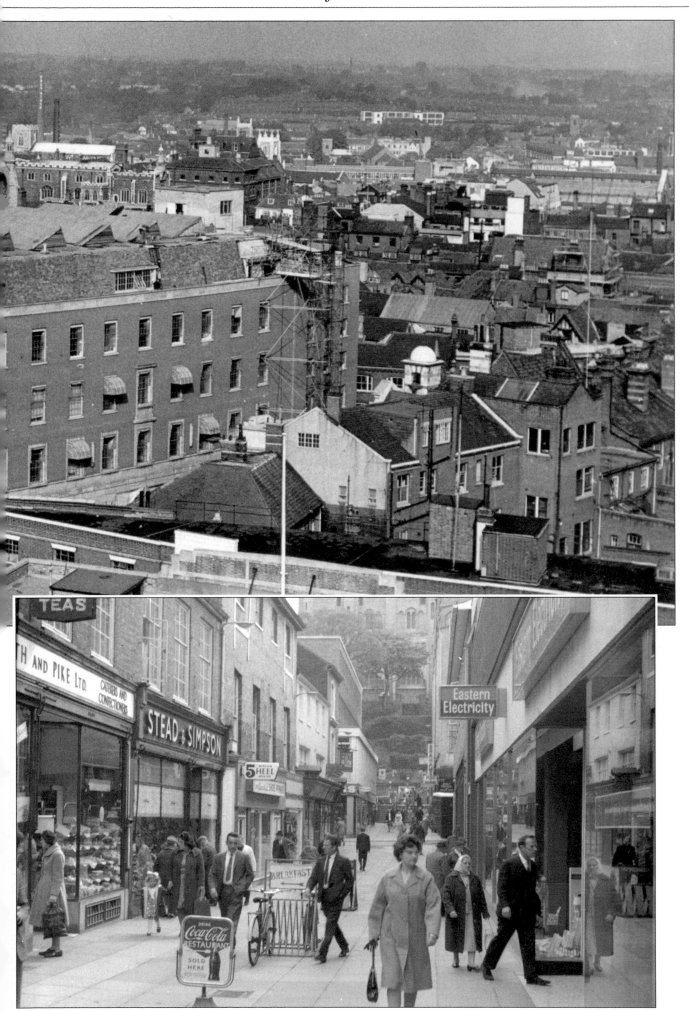

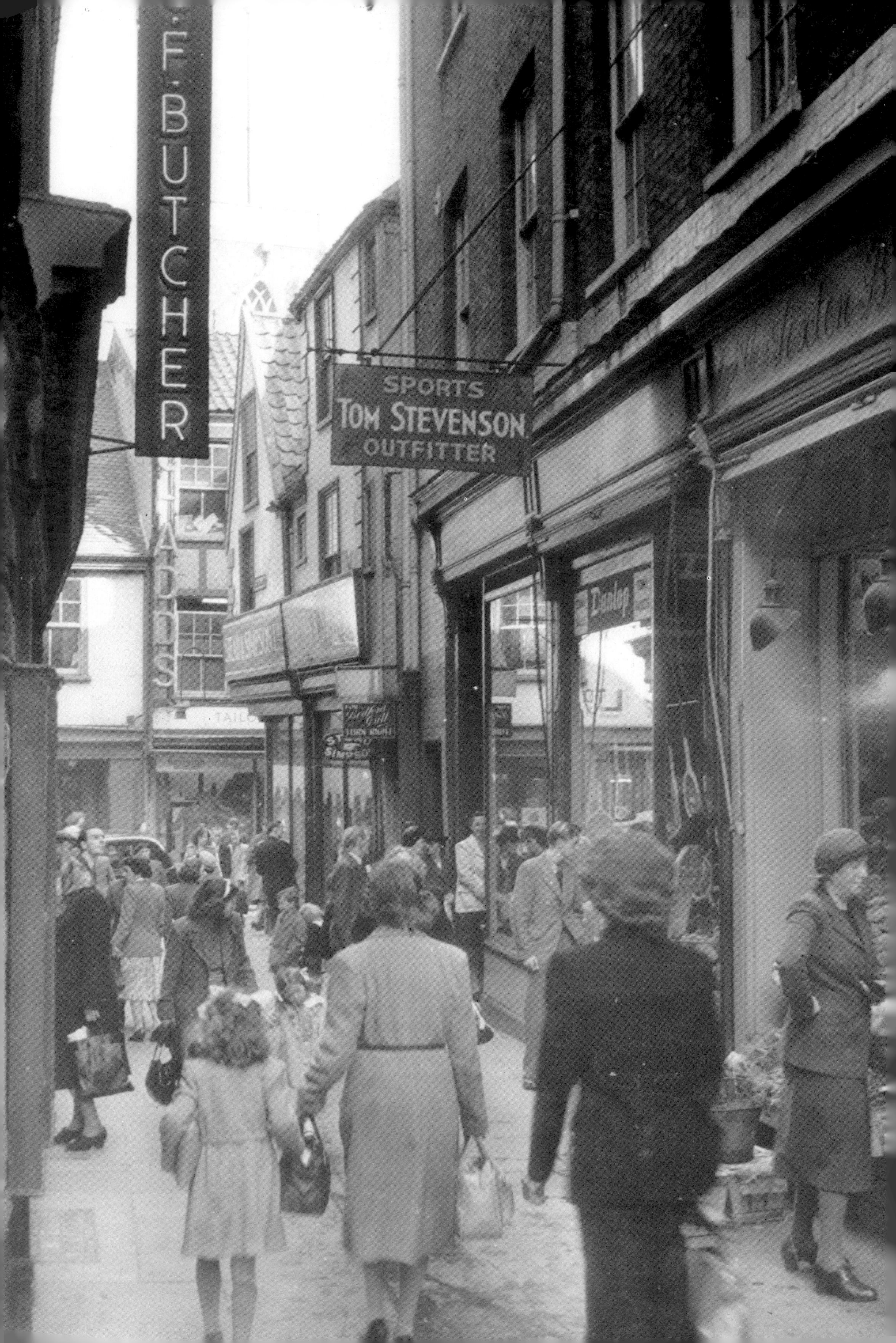
F. BUTCHER
SPORTS
TOM STEVENSON
OUTFITTER
Dunlop

Left: Compared to the austere years following the end of the second world war, the early part of the 1950s saw more choice in the shops and the eventual end of all rationing in Britain. This photograph dates from 1953, and the people featured here experienced 'proper shopping' at first hand as they promenaded along the narrow streets of Norwich looking for the best buys. A note on the back of the original print describes local shopping areas as 'having narrow alleys where wheeled traffic may not pass' but adds a hint of criticism: 'recent shop fronts spoil some of the fine old buildings.' We could be forgiven for thinking that it is only modern folk who look back wistfully on days gone by, but the truth is that nostalgia has been with us for a long as there has been change in the world - and long may it continue!

Above: A busy Saturday afternoon in Curls Department Store is shown in this picture which dates from the early 1950s. At the time, Curls was one of five department stores in Norwich. During the war Curls' five-storey building had been destroyed in the infamous Baedeker air raids of 1942. The directors of the company acquired temporary premises in order to create continuity for their business, their customers and their employees. Retailing provided employment for 12 per cent of the local workforce at the time this picture was taken. Shop opening hours were much more limited then than they are today, with Saturdays being a frenzy of activity accounting for a third of each week's takings in the big stores.

The sights, sounds and smells of open-air market trading are brought to life by this delightful picture which dates from the early 1950s. A note on the back of the original print describes the composition as 'Spring Flowers in the Norwich Produce Market'. Familiar retail names can be seen in the background - J Lyons and Company and H Samuel, the best-known jewellers in the country.

At work

The contractors, Gill & Son, did good business in helping to restore and rebuild the city after the Luftwaffe had done with it. The shell of the new Curl's store is almost finished. It was the 'new' store because it was being put up after the old one had been hammered during the Blitz. In a small matter of months the scaffolding would be down and people could return to shop in the bright new surroundings of one of the city's premier stores. The bus is heading along Red Lion Street towards Castle Meadow. In the 1990s down there you would find the new Castle Mall Shopping Centre. To the left of Curl's is Rampant Horse Street. Surely this name must be almost unique amongst any city's streets. Quite what the horse was rampant about is not related. The name comes quite simply from that of the old Rampant Horse Inn. There was once a flourishing horse market here. Animals for farm work would be brought to the sales and auctions, given the once over by knowing farmers. They would feel their hocks and check their teeth and put in an appropriate bid. The more genteel came to see if a good hunter or a quiet, but sturdy, pony for the trap could be bought. The smells and sights of the horse fair were replaced in this view by the sound of the pneumatic drill and the sweet smell of success for the future.

A glance at the 1950s

MELODY MAKERS
Few teenage girls could resist the blatant sex-appeal of 'Elvis the Pelvis', though their parents were scandalised at the moody Presley's provocatively gyrating hips. The singer took America and Britain by storm with such hits as 'Jailhouse Rock', 'All Shook Up' and 'Blue Suede Shoes'. The rhythms of Bill Haley and his Comets, Buddy Holly, Chuck Berry, and Roy Orbison (who had a phenomenal three-octave voice) turned the 1950s into the Rock 'n' Roll years.

INVENTION AND TECHNOLOGY
Until the late 1950s you did not carry radios around with you. Radios were listened to at home, plugged into a mains socket in every average sitting room. Japan was in the forefront of electronic developments even then, and in 1957 the Japanese company Sony introduced the world's very first all-transistor radio - an item of new technology that was small enough to fit into your pocket. The major consumer product caught on fast - particularly with teenage listeners.

SCIENCE AND DISCOVERY
DNA (deoxyribonucleic acid) was first defined as long ago as 1953, and the effects have been far-reaching. The key discovery was developed over the following years and today DNA finger-printing has become an accepted part of life. Genetic diseases such as haemophilia and cystic fibrosis have been identified. Criminals are contin-ually detected and brought to justice. Biological drugs have been developed. Drought and disease-resistant plants have been engineered - and more controversially Dolly the sheep has been produced.

The City Hall, at the top of the picture, had only been open for four years when the German bombers arrived over Norwich. The area around Orford Place had its heart ripped out. Although the city had been hit earlier in the year, Vauxhall Street being badly affected, it was on successive nights in late April 1942 that the major offensive occurred. Hitler launched what were called the Baedeker raids. These were named after the 19th century German writer who launched the series of Baedeker travel guides. Allied bombing had hit the

Baltic harbour town of Lubeck and destroyed some of its best architecture. In revenge, Hitler ordered reprisal raids on historic British cities, the sort that would appear in the guide book. The bombardment was relentless. In total, 14,000 homes were damaged and 1,200 completely destroyed. Beer from Morgan's brewery flowed down Synagogue Street like an alcoholic flood tide. Gas mains ruptured and the Midland & Great Northern Joint Railway's city station on Barn Road was destroyed. After the first raids many residents fled the city into the countryside. The death toll was reduced, thanks to this foresight. Looking back, one can understand the bombing of strategic targets. It is hard to come to terms, though, with the deliberate and systematic destruction of churches, galleries and monuments. But, has anyone learned the lesson? As the 20th century drew to a close, over half a century on from this picture, European skies were, once again, home to bombers flying missions in the name of peace.

Above: This little piece of Norwich is not one of its most attractive sites or sights. No picture of a roller, wheelbarrow or man leaning on a shovel can provoke too many romantic thoughts. Here, on this corner of St Giles Street, the picture hasn't become any more attractive over the years. It is still the City Hall car park, but it has never been big enough to cater for anything like the volume of car drivers wishing to visit the local government offices. Across the city, other car parking areas and multi-storey buildings have had to be developed to meet the motoring demands of the second half of the 20th century. A mixture of pedestrian only streets, a one way system and the creation of the ring road have helped to keep things on the move. More recently, some of the roads into Norwich have had bus and taxi only lanes decreed. This has been an attempt to speed up public transport and to encourage drivers to abandon cars as the means of getting to work or to shop. In the picture, the line of bicycles leaning against the wall suggests that 40 years ago some people had heeded the environmental message, or, perhaps, they couldn't afford a car. Nowadays, some of the city's roads have cycle paths and lanes marked on them. There has been some increase in the use of pedal power. Some special routes around the city have been set up, including Marston Lane, along the Yare valley, Drayton path and the old M & GN Railway path, following the River Wensum.

Above right: Bethel Street was once called Upper Newport. It got its present name from Bethel Hospital, founded by a Mrs Chapman in 1713. She aimed for it to deal with lunatics and not natural fools. The name would have been inspired by London's 13th century asylum, the Bethlehem Royal Hospital, which became known as Bedlam. Mrs Chapman's hospital was enlarged in Victorian times, but it is not that which takes centre stage in this photograph. The Central Library is about to rise above these concrete foundations. Reinforcing rods and box girders will soon hold together the

floors of learning and the books, papers and archives that are the basis of any well-stocked library. It is more than a place to come and get your latest racy Jilly Cooper novel or another of Catherine Cookson's historical tales of love and misfortune in Northumbria. The library provides a place of retreat for people who want to escape for an hour or two and lose themselves in the printed word. Researchers find a store of local history in the archive documents. Old newspapers can be brought up on screen, so that long forgotten incidents can be read over again. With the addition of computer technology, fast searches for material can be made without needing to look in every nook and cranny of the building. Unfortunately, Central Library's stay here was to be short-lived. In 1994, a simple fault in a lighting starter motor caused a short and an electrical fire began. By the time it was discovered, the building was well alight and could not be saved. Temporary premises on Anglia Square, at the back of the Odeon Cinema, now house the reference section, with the lending library sitting on Ber Street in the old Glasswells building.

Below: You can't computerise everything. This is one scene from the 1950s which is going to be with us for some time. The lights might last longer, but they will still need to be changed from time to time. Here, the council workforce is servicing the street lamps from its state of the art mobile tower. Health and safety was not as potent a force then. That tower has a lean not unlike that of a certain other one in Pisa. Did the workman stay up there as the whole contraption moved from lamp to lamp? It wouldn't happen now. Climb down every time or face disciplinary action will be the instruction now. In addition, don't forget your hard hat. Presumably, that's in case a very heavy 100 watt bulb falls on top of you. In the meantime, while he's up there he could do a spot of dusting. There's bound to be the odd cobweb lurking around. The householder behind the lamppost probably preferred to have the lamp left as it was.

The gleam of the sodium falling into the bedroom wasn't the best sort of lullaby to send you off to sleep. Looking back to times when there were gas lamps, this photograph reminds us that there was the job of the lamplighter, who lit the mantles every night with the help of a long pole. Maybe he was the same chap who came back at the crack of dawn with that same pole to knock us up to go to work. Now, then, what was that joke about how many council workmen did it take to change a light bulb?

Bottom: These two chaps are not taking part in some version of the 'Generation Game'. They cannot see what the other is doing, tucked away in their little cubicles and you might think it is some sort of competition. However, they have not watched an expert work on the television sets until they were working perfectly and then been told to fine tune them just as well. These men are the experts, themselves. In their white coats they are as much like scientists as a chemist in a laboratory. Theirs is just as exact a science. Pictured in the old workshop at Blofield Heath, a few miles east of Norwich off the A47, the engineers of the RC Snelling Company come to grips with the now outdated 405 line system. They would move on to work on 625 lines and through to the mysteries of satellite and digital TV. Ivor, seen on the left, worked for the company for many years until around 1990. He saw some changes in those years from valves to transistors and from black and white to colour. The man on the right, with the Buddy Holly glasses that were all the rage in the late 50s and early 60s, is Mr Hedley. He went on to become the firm's managing director. He would be able to hold up his head in meetings as one who had seen it, done it and not only got the T shirt, but the business suit to prove it. Any young whipper-snapper in the workforce who questioned his practical knowledge only needed to be shown this photograph to realise that not all managers have graduated to the boardroom from Oxford. There are plenty more who have studied at the university of life.

It's a sunny day, nice for flying over the river meandering to the east of the city centre. The blobs in the middle spoil the peaceful scene. The gasholders, to give them their proper name, have the appearance of massive snare drums. Buddy Rich or Eric Delaney might have been passing and dropped them off there. Most people call them gasometers, but that description should be kept for measuring the gas. Let's not be too picky, there's plenty more to talk about here. Riverside Rd runs along the Wensum. A line of boats packs the riverbank as people are taking to the water for a happy day's outing. Around Pull's Ferry is a busy place for the yachting and sailing fraternity. It is here that you can find the 15th century watergate that takes you to Cathedral Close. On the right hand side of the river there's a lovely walk, leading down and away past the north of the city. Holding your lover's hand and gazing at the flotilla on the water is a romantic way to spend a summer's evening. Just as long as you don't look too far over at those iron and steel monstrosities, or the magic of the moment will be lost.

Snaking up to the right, on this June day in 1972, is Rosary Road. Gas Hill and the parallel road of Kett's Hill lead away towards the Great Yarmouth road. Named after the rebel, Robert Ketts, not surprisingly, this road leads to the city prison.

Have you got a PC with five gigs of hard drive space, 64 megs of RAM and a 32 speed CD-ROM? Add to that a laser printer, fax-modem and desktop scanner and these ladies would not have a clue what it was you were asking. Yet, they were working on the very same subject, if only they knew it. This is the computer room in the City Treasurer's Department. Although there are cables, wires and gadgets all over, it is as far removed from the information technology at the dawn of the 21st century as riding a bike is to space travel. The ribbon of computer tape and the machinery it is being fed through look more as if the operator is passing something through a mangle. We aren't quite on the information super highway just yet, are we ladies? Yet, these will be the people who will retrain and be compiling statistics on their databases and accessing multi-user files in years to come. By the end of the 1990s the majority of homes have a computer and little children use them as happily as anyone else; more happily, in some cases. It may come as a surprise to realise that it was as long ago as the 1830s that Londoner Charles Babbage developed plans for an analytical engine, the forerunner of the modern digital computer. His notebooks lay forgotten for a hundred years. Even then, it was not until the late 1950s and early 1960s that people like Noyce and Kilby in California's Silicon Valley were able to develop the integrated circuit microchip. When Intel produced the first ever microprocessor in 1971, the computer age, as we know it, was ready to explode, though it would be another 20 years before it really went 'bang'. Now then, I've got to take my mouse to the web, or I think that's what my five year old told me to do.

Cottages, Cinemas and Air Stations

The de-population of rural areas has usually benefited the towns to which country people moved. Norwich has gained immeasurably from a business started in the 1860s by a farmer's son named Charles Gill. In the 1860s he and his half brother, John Youngs, set up as speculative builders of terraced cottages. As these were beyond the pocket of those destined to live in them, entire rows were sold to landlords who rented them out to working families for around a shilling (5p) a week. As they probably cost £30 or so pounds to build each one, it was a long term investment to await a profit. By comparison Army officers then paid a similar sum to ship their wives out to India.

The business worked initially in the Unthank Road area of Norwich, building durable dwellings for long term investors, hence the expression 'as safe as houses'. In time J Youngs set up the contracting business known today as Youngs Builders.

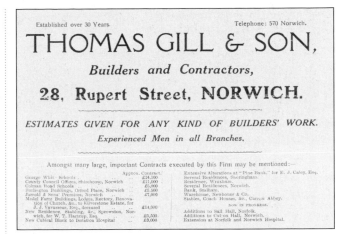

Established over 30 Years.   Telephone: 570 Norwich.

THOMAS GILL & SON,
Builders and Contractors,
28, Rupert Street, NORWICH.

ESTIMATES GIVEN FOR ANY KIND OF BUILDERS' WORK.
Experienced Men in all Branches.

The builders yard was originally in Rupert Street until destroyed by a wartime bomb. Thomas Gill joined his father's business which he carried on and established as the firm known today. It was the period in which town and county councils were taking on new duties which had formerly been undertaken by public spirited gentlemen, other local benefactors and a medley of parish councils and charitable bodies.

Above left: *Charles Gill, founder of the company.*
Above right: *An early advertisement for the builders service.* ***Below:*** *The company's transport was lent for a Sunday School outing to Lakenham circa 1905 (picture from a contemporary postcard).*

The Education Act of 1870 had laid responsibility for constructing and maintaining schools firmly on the shoulders of local councillors, which resulted in many lucrative contracts for local builders. In 1910 for example Gills took on the building of two schools for a total of £19,000, an enormous sum equivalent to over a £million today.

Above: Restoration and underpinning of the Cow Tower on Riverside, carried out in the early 1950s.
Top: The staff of T Gill & Son in a picture from the 1930s. Mr Sidney Gill is on the extreme left.

The old town councils had operated their small enterprises from town halls built in an age when public administration was regarded as an unwelcome and costly intrusion into the private lives of independent Englishmen.

Shire House in Norwich was built in an expansive and prosperous age when public buildings were generously proportioned and handsomely designed by the best architects and builders of the brilliant Edwardian era. Commercial enterprises such as Jarrolds the printers were free-spending customers as were the great estate owners such as JJ Vavassour Esq. who spent the vast sum of £14,000 on model farm buildings, gate lodges for estate staff homes plus a new Rectory and restoration work to the church which served his Kilverstone Estate. The independent hospitals which raised funds from public donations were not infrequent clients of Gills in an age when doctors subsidised their poorer patients by charging higher fees to those who could afford them.

One of the most notable Gill buildings is the beautiful 1926 Barclays Bank, built in the popular Lutyenesque Queen Anne style, which occupies the historic Gurney Bank site on Bank Plain. The cleverly concealed electric lighting was then considered revolutionary while locals dubbed the building 'Versailles' from its Mansard roofline.

The Great Depression put millions out of work while those who had jobs turned to the silver screen to escape the reality outside. In Norfolk, the more prosperous estates were able to farm work out to builders and contractors whereas many smaller farms had little choice but to let things slide between the wars until they were needed once more by a desperate nation. During this difficult decade Gills survived thanks to the enormous public demand for local cinemas within reach of a bus or train journey. Picture Houses were built by Gills in Cromer, North Walsham, Sheringham, Swaffham and Wells to cater for a rural, and holiday, population in outlying coastal towns. The company also built the Regal in Norwich which, like many town cinemas, provided knife and fork high teas for families who had come to town for their weekly outing.

During the years of awakening, when Britain at last recognised the threat of war, Gills participated towards the national defence by building a number of Royal Airforce Stations in the flat landscape of East Anglia. There were many other wartime contracts on coastal locations built to watch out for possible invasion from the sea. Military encampments were laid out for equipping and training allied troops who had escaped from all the occupied countries of Europe to continue the fight for freedom at our side. They were joined in the second year of the war by the generously provisioned soldiers and airmen of the tremendously wealthy USA who made such a mark on traditional British society.

Following final victory the nation set to work to rebuild its damaged towns, factories, ports and railway stations. Once the enormous problems caused by rationing supply and transport facilities had been resolved there was a building boom which changed the face of towns and countryside alike. New housing estates and retirement homes provided better homes for those who had lost or left their old ones. The clean lines of contemporary architecture were everywhere apparent as Gills joined the nation's builders in erecting swimming pools and factories, hospitals and schools to cater for the post war 'baby boom'.

One of the most outstanding buildings of this era is the department store built for Curls which is now occupied by a branch of Debenhams. This was followed by the GPO building in Pottergate, while the opening of the Norfolk and Norwich Hospital Maternity Wing was honoured by HM the Queen Mother, whose younger daughter opened the Orthopaedic block.. During this decade Sydney's son Thomas steered the firm firmly back to building houses in addition to undertaking substantial contract work on what have become modern landmarks. The work on the Rotunda in Norwich Castle contrasts with the clear span open space of Bally's Shoe Factory to show the breadth of tasks undertaken by Gills.

Today the Company remains essentially a traditional, local, family-run business. Apprentices still learn traditional skills. But techniques change, methods of procurement alter, new types of building evolve. Only by adapting to new ideas and embracing new skills can the Company remain up to date, competitive and vibrant. Everything old was new once. Today's new skill will be tomorrow's 'tradition'. The Company is always looking to the future so as to keep its history safe.

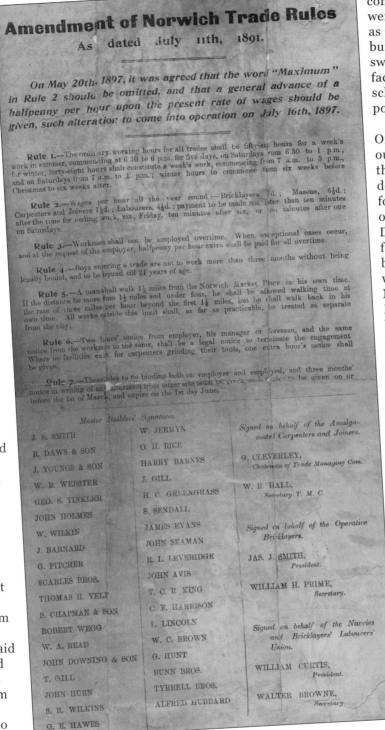

Above: *The Working Rule of 1891.*

You'll find Snellings below the 100 foot mast

Snellings are different and proud of it. What's more thousands of satisfied customers keep them going. People expect to hunt for lawn mower specialists out in the country, not to mention boat builders in the Broads, but not a Television showroom and service centre. Ever since Roy Snelling started in 1954 every piece of promotional paper has carried the same clear map showing people where to find his business. He's still there!

R C Snelling, now the biggest TV rental and sales company between Norwich and the sea, was built on faith in the future and a keen understanding of product and clientele. The saga began in 1938, two years after the young Billy Butlin set up his first revolutionary holiday camp, when 14 year old Roy Snelling, mad keen on the wireless, started his apprenticeship with a Wireless Technician. It was then the brave new world of the 1930s when the Wireless was at the cutting edge of technology and the Great Depression was fading into memory except in the old heavy industry based towns of the North, . Although private pilots still navigated

Below: *Early television repairs.*

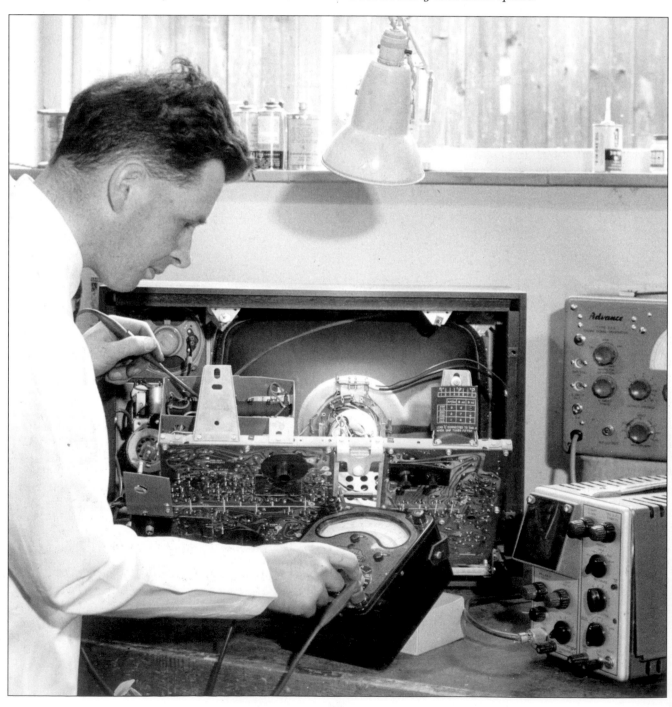

and Mechanical Engineers (REME), known to generations of soldiers as Ruin Everything Mechanical Eventually.

Although a Hostilities Only National Serviceman he was not discharged until 1947 when he returned to his original employers to repair the wireless sets which, with gramophones, comprised the ultimate in home entertainment for a growing audience.

As more and more homes aspired to the wireless sets which had formed part of wartime factory and barracks life Roy Snelling aspired to run his own show in catering for the market of the future.

In 1954 the thirty year old Roy Snelling, supported by his mother, grasped the nettle and bought his first premises for his new business. The redundant Victorian laundry of Blofield Hall was purchased for £400, then over a year's pay for many people. In the first three months he took a total of £8 at a time when shop assistants and office staff were starting work on around £2 a week. His critics laughed at someone hoping to attract business away from a town to a hut lacking a shop window in a village with infrequent bus services.

their aircraft and the services were following suit as fast as funds allowed.

The Wireless was definitely part of the future and a wise choice for an ambitious lad keen to acquire a worthwhile trade. Not unexpectedly that assured well planned world came to an end with the outbreak of World War Two in 1939. The modernised forces snapped up every skilled wireless operator and mechanic available to operate signals sections and to train new entrants. Roy Snelling, in common with hundreds of others like him, was left in the lurch to carry on as best he could using books and manuals to learn his trade. As soon as he became 18 the Army took over his training following which he served in the Royal Electrical

Shoppers today are glad to avoid, whenever possible, the transport and shopping hassles that go with living in the country and going to any large town for supplies. A visit to

Above: *Part of the showroom in the 1960s.*
Top: *A demonstration of the latest television models in the early 1960s.*

Snellings below the 100 foot mast involves a drive through pleasant country with ample free car parking by the shop door and a choice that rivals any major town showroom. The one thing that has not changed since the days of the old laundry forty odd years ago is the standard of service which comes from a company whose reins are still handled by its founder.

To achieve this Roy Snelling worked with all the passion and enthusiasm of the conscientious pioneer. He worked seven days a week, usually for sixteen hours at stretch, to turn his personal dream into reality, aided and abetted by his mother who fed and watered him as he built up his business. Early publicity leaflets invited the public to consider installing a TV receiving set for which he offered the first class service of one with fifteen years expertise. He further pointed out the advantages of TV as the cheapest form of entertainment on offer and asked people to leave messages as he was regularly out and about

serving his customers. He married in 1965 and gladly delegated the growing office work to his capable partner who joined him in working 'til late at night..

Roy Snelling still believes that the customer is king although he no longer needs to visit them himself to repair sets at ten at night at the end of a busy day driving and adjusting. Modern viewers can have no conception of the rather hazy pictures that came through the air waves to the 405 line TV sets in rural districts at a distance from the very few early TV transmission masts. The word got around that the best man in Norfolk to achieve success in the difficult art of persuading pictures to appear and coalesce was Roy Snelling. Among his happier memories are those oft repeated occasions when he installed a household's first

Above: An advertisement from when television was first introduced to the British public.
Top: The kitchen appliance range in the 1960s.

TWO MODELS
of proved value
from a wide range
in the Showroom

PYE VT. 4
14" Table Model for BBC and
Commercial Programmes
PRICE 67 gns. Tax Paid

FERGUSON 992
14" Table Model
PRICE 59 gns. Tax Paid

ever TV and watched the joyous wonder blaze across his clients' faces as the visible world came into their living room.

When Roy Snelling broke new ground as a TV supplier and repair man families had no need to argue or to have their own sets in different rooms to see their favourite programmes, the choice was made for you. Quite simply it was BBC TV switched on or BBC TV switched off. When the first commercial programmes appeared on ITV institutions such as clubs, barracks and residential hotels and retirement homes often went to the expense of providing for inmates two television rooms respectively labelled the BBC Room and the ITV Room. In those days long before every tourist expected a TV set in every bedroom murder was a distinct possibility whenever someone tried to change the channel.

The smaller sets of today are worked by ingenious printed circuits which have superseded the friable glass valves, like lamp bulbs, which were the bane of everyone's lives bar the suppliers. The tiny tools now used need a keen eye, aided by a jeweller's mounted magnifying glass, and a steady hand to

top the training and knowledge which has turned electrical repair work into something like dentistry. Not surprisingly each speciality, be it TV, videos, satellite or Hi-Fi, has its own workshop manned by master specialists who are not distracted by attempting to be a Jack of all trades and master of none. Should clients require any type of aerial installed or serviced a call to the Snelling switch board will be immediately transferred by radio telephone to a well chosen sub-contractor ready to give the same rapid response that customers expect from East Anglia's premier TV engineers.

Country people still lack the capability to tap into cable TV available to townees just as in the days when they continued to use oil lamps up until the 1950s and 60s long after town dwellers accepted electricity as the norm. They can, however, benefit from the Star Wars technology developed during the super-nations race into space by fixing a satellite dish to their wall to receive signals that have travelled a distance equal to circumnavigating planet earth twice. Wherever you live within the Snelling orbit you are guaranteed a service engineer arriving to effect repairs to your equipment within a few hours of your call.

Above: An early advertisement.
Right and below: The premises in the 1970s.

 Most jobs can be finished at the customer' home or business while rental clients can be supplied with a replacement at no extra charge.

Townsmen and villagers alike, in their 60s, have memories of tradesmen's horse-drawn delivery carts and vans when milk was ladelled out of 17 gallon churns into jugs held by housewives and children standing at the roadside. The same people can select from thirty odd TV programmes which have been transmitted into space and bounced back off satellites, rotating like mechanical moons, to give a clearer picture and sound than possible along close to ground air waves. Snellings can either provide a modern TV capable of receiving such signals at video level or adapt your TV-Video combination to accept space reflected signals.

Now it's all taken for granted just as postage stamps and steam trains became within a generation of their beginning. Definitely not taken for granted by Roy Snelling are his staff of over thirty including Hedley Watts and two other Originals from the 50s. Hedley Watts, now Managing Director, joined as an Apprentice in 1958 at about the same time that Mrs Snelling gave her bank book to her son with the words 'Here's my bank book, I don't want it back.'. Of these well spent funds no doubt one of the early investments was the two way radio system for the delivery and service van which enabled the hard pressed owner to keep ahead of competition by reducing journey times wasted on returning to base and reaching customers earlier than expected.

Customers have always been offered the choice between rental and purchase of all equipment stocked by

Below and right: *The premises today.*

Snellings of Blofield. It is unusual to find a TV rental company that sticks to agreed prices for the term of the rent period with the householder. Hotels, Conference Centres and Businesses find the Snelling rental package a valuable tool which can be enhanced or replaced soon after despatching a message by any communications method including state of the art Prestel. Ever since their pioneering use of radio vans Snellings have trusted the most modern communications methods to help serve their customers. Spare parts ordered by Prestel minimise unacceptable delays in repairs and so enhance turn around, keep customers happy and reduce overheads to the benefit of profits.

The showrooms provide separate viewing areas for customers who like the latest functional look of plastic, aluminium and skeletal legs for their TV and Hi-Fi kit and those who share a Victorian outlook that TVs, like table legs, should be decently hidden. The latter are well catered for by an appropriately wall papered showroom full of elegantly

veneered and inlaid pieces of furniture in which the most fully equipped entertainment centres are ensconced ready to pop out at the flick of a switch to the amazement of any Regency lady who would otherwise have felt at home there.

Thirty or so years ago colour sets were prohibitively costly and so complicated that an engineer was needed to make the 17 adjustments necessary to obtain a good picture. Currently the commonplace colour set requires only five adjustments and by the millennium it will be down to one made by the viewer. Those who remember the old long tubes and small screens can be forgiven for wondering why TVs still occupy the same floor area as before when they are so flat. It is hard to recall that early screen were less than half the size of those in use now.

Television has become part of almost everyone's lives to such an extent that people can now control it by the use of videos to record programmes put out when they are at work, in the gym or socialising and still enjoy the programmes that they select to fit in with their lifestyle. The exciting world of video games and the discs offering 36 volume encyclopaedias in your hand belong to the era envisaged by HG Wells' and every other Sci-Fi author whose imagination soared ahead of man's inventive and constructive capabilities.

Snellings cater for the area within a thirty mile radius of their famous mast offering the same good value in technology and service alike to the Hi-Fi buffs who talk

Above: The modern reception area.
Right: Roy Snelling, founder of the company.

knowledgeably about building up systems which employ digital recording and graphic equalisers to tailor the total quality of equipment to a customers ear and environment as they do to the tone deaf whose elderly sets are happily rusted onto their one favourite station. In either case quality of engineering at prices to suit the free spender and those temporarily fiscally impaired is of the essence in maintaining customer loyalty.

As loyalty is a two way medium in which partners rely on each other Roy Snelling turned the company which he and his wife laboured to create into a charitable trust to protect the employment future of the 38 staff and to ensure continuity of service for the tens of thousands of customers who rely on Snellings of Blofield.

City's technical excellence

Part of the character of Norwich, as we approach the end of the 20th century, comes from its thriving student community; with its many educational institutions, not least among which is City College, the modern city of Norwich boasts an excellent range of educational provision at all levels.

At the turn of the last century, however, the story was rather different. Technical education was a relatively new concept, and Norwich's first technical school, the institution which was to become City College, had been established for less than a decade. Housed originally on the top floor of a building in St George's Bridge Street, it had been set up in 1891, as a starting point for a Central Technical School, in response to growing concern all over England at the nation's widespread lack of trained labour. Mr H C Bolingbroke, whom many people credit with having begun the movement, thought that one of the shortcomings of the education system as it stood was that 'there was a great deal done in the schools for the head and but little to train the hands.' The purpose

of the city's new technical school, then, was to provide technical education, but as Mr Wild, the Deputy Mayor of Norwich in 1991, explained at inauguration of the new school, this did not mean teaching the specific skills and practices of any one particular trade, but had as its aim more general objectives, such as 'to stimulate the student to understand the reason for all the simple problems of work' and to effect 'a greater sympathy of action between Head, Hand and Eye'. The notion seems to have been akin to today's concept of transferable skills - by helping the workman to learn 'the principles of science and art applicable to industries' and to understand the properties of his materials and their applications, an adaptable workforce would be created, who would then be well equipped to learn any trade.

Above: *The Eastern Daily Press report of the opening of the new technical college in 1891.*
Above left: *Alderman Sir George White MP.*
Below: *An early woodworking class.*

Drawing, it was felt, should be the basis of all technical instruction, so a special area was set aside for this in the room at St George's Bridge Street; also in the room were ten benches, each providing workspace for four boys, and stands for twelve carvers. To begin with, only 'recreative technical evening classes' were held, providing instruction in drawing, carpentry, carving and cabinet-making not only to boys but also to mature students, or seniors, as they were termed. There was an important role for the new school new college to play in the future economic development of the area. Norwich was, in 1891, suffering badly from the effects of the industrial revolution; the textile industry which had brought prosperity to the city in the earlier part of the century had all but disappeared, and until new industries could be established, poverty and squalor were rife. By the end of the century economic recovery had begun, with boot and shoe manufacturing providing a new source of income and, together with the food and drink industry, engineering, printing and building, forming the basis of Norwich's new economy. All these new crafts were reflected in the prospectus of courses offered by the embryonic technical school, which was very soon re-located in Bethel Street where in 1893 it began to offer day classes as well as evening courses.

Despite some initial resistance by traditional artisans to the notion that a trade education could be received anywhere other than in the workplace, the school continued to develop and by 1901 it had moved into the Municipal Technical Institute in St George's Street. In addition to science, art, domestic science, manual training and trade classes, courses were offered in preparation for London University examinations, while at another building in Duke Street commercial and

literacy classes were held, though Duke Street, in its early days, did have the disadvantage that when it rained students 'were obliged to keep moving their desks about, or else they stood in a pool of water'. By 1905 students could take a four year course which would give them 'a thorough technical training in dealing with the intricacies of Home and Foreign Trade' and 'that mental alertness and intellectual development so necessary for grappling with the problems of modern commerce'.

The first world war limited the college's activities, but in the years between the wars expansion continued, as the climate was supportive of technical education and training; a new range of trade qualifications became available, and day-release for apprentices became a widespread practice. The boot and shoe industry remained at the core of the college's curriculum, but engineering also began to feature heavily, with motor vehicle maintenance, electrical engineering, and courses of relevance to the printing and construction industries. In 1919 the Junior Technical School began its intensive two-year course which prepared youngsters for entry to the trades and professions, and it was not until 1958 that this was discontinued.

During the second world war, many jobs were filled by previously unskilled workers, and a whole series of short courses were run to teach the emergency workforce, which included many women, the requisite skills. The college fostered an entrepreneurial spirit, and was prepared to run any course for which it perceived a

Above: *Moving from St George Street to Ipswich Road in the 1940s.*

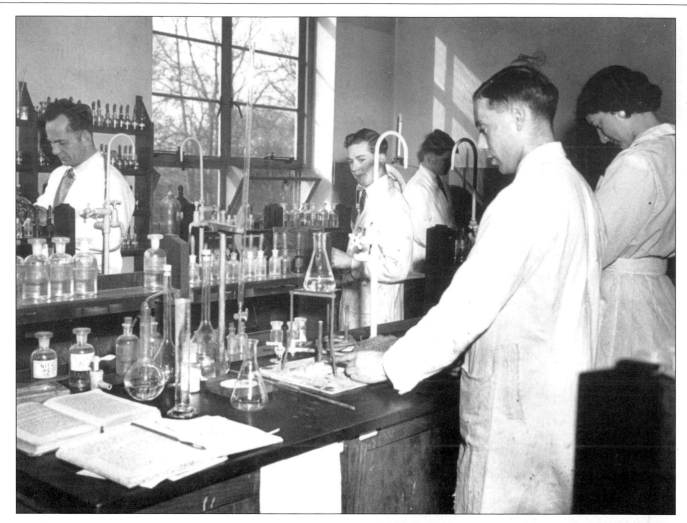

demand; in 1938, for example, it ran a course for milkmen, covering all aspects of handling and processing milk. This spirit still reigns today, with the college providing, amongst other things, a successful 'Learning to Retire' course.

In 1953 the new building of Norwich City College and Art School, as it was then, was officially opened; this three-storey building, with a frontage fifty feet longer than Norwich's City Hall, was the first college of its kind to be completed since the end of the war. Since then, the building programme has continued and the Ipswich Road campus has grown and adapted to keep up with demand: workshops, a new refectory; a new sports hall - which meant that the existing gymnasium could become a theatre, thus allowing the existing hall to be turned into the library; the Hotel School; the Business School; and most recently, the Norfolk Building - housing new construction and engineering workshops.

City College now offers in excess of 800 courses from basic skills through to postgraduate study across a range of vocational, academic and leisure subjects. The areas of business, management and computing have seen significant expansion in recent years and the college's Hotel School is recognised as one of the best in the country.

Top: *A practical chemistry class in 1958.*
Above: *The Norfolk Building at City College, opened in 1998.*

The college has broadened its appeal to include more and more people in learning from all walks of life and strives to ensure that disability or learning difficulties are no barrier to a college education. It now enrols over 20,000 students a year, over half of whom are over the age of 25.

Several of these have gone on to distinguished careers in sporting, academic or public life, or the arts; one former student who will be known to most people today is actor and entertainer Stephen Fry.

It would have been impossible for those present at the inauguration of the institution more than a hundred years

City College NORWICH

tunities to all sections of the community. To further this it manages The Learning Shop on Guildhall Hill to offer advice about learning. Opened in May 1997 it welcomed over 20,000 visitors in its first year. Another new initiative is the e-Commerce Centre in Theatre Street. Part of the Norfolk and Norwich Millennium project, it will provide computing courses on the latest technology.

ago to envisage just how much the college would expand, although the trend towards expansion was certainly there from the very outset. The 50 junior and 50 seniors who attended night school in 1891 had become 870 students on day and evening courses by 1895; by 1948 there were 5,000 students in total, including Juniors and Art students; by 1965 the number had risen to over 7,500, excluding Juniors and Art students. The college seems to have begun to attract significant numbers of students from outside the immediate area during the years before the second world war, when some ten per cent came from the county; by 1948 some 33 per cent were county students, and by 1965 the balance had swayed, with more than 50 per cent of student population coming from the county. Since the 1950s, a significant number of international students have chosen to study at City College; amongst the countries represented here at various times are Nigeria, Iran, Malaysia and Thailand, and the college has forged links with the University of Lagos and the University of Ibadan.

However, the role which City College plays within the community today is not far removed from the one which its founders envisaged for it and brings learning oppor-

Increasingly the college is taking education out into the community through a programme of outreach projects at centres across the county.

When the dedication stone of the Ipswich Road building was unveiled in 1953, more than half a century after the institution began, the college affirmed its commitment to 'the enrichment of the life of Norwich', and this commitment is still very strong in City College. The life of Norwich has changed, and other educational institutions have grown up alongside it, but City College has a very special role to play, one that is important to the community it serves and one that it will continue to fulfill in the most appropriate way as it enters its third century of existence.

Above left: The state-of-the-art computer aided learning centre. Top left: A 'cookery lesson' from Albert Roux at the College's public restaurant. Top right: The College logo. Below: The Princess Royal's visit to open the Norfolk Building in 1998.

No one protects more

Norwich Union has been protecting its customers against risk for over 200 years, and throughout this time it has occupied a place at the very heart of the Norwich community. Its founder was Thomas Bignold, a city wine merchant who wisely tried to take out insurance against the threat from highwaymen during his move from Kent to Norwich, but was unable to find anyone who would insure him. Perceiving that there was a need for this kind of insurance, Bignold formed the Norwich General Insurance Company in 1792 and went on to form the Norwich Union Fire Insurance Society five years later. The Norwich Union Life Insurance Society was founded in 1808, and it was this branch which much later, in 1925, took over the fire insurance company. Five generations of the Bignold family presided over Norwich Union affairs from the founding of the company until the retirement of Sir Robert Bignold in 1964, and the Bignold family name lives on in Norwich through the Bignold school situated in the heart of the city.

Throughout its 200-year history, Norwich Union has contributed to the social and economic well-being of both the city of Norwich and the county of Norfolk. During the 19th century Samuel Bignold, Thomas's youngest son, served the city both as Mayor and as MP, and the tradition of service to the community has been continued throughout the 20th century by the company's employees, many of whom also served their country during the two world wars.

Thomas Bignold was firmly committed to providing opportunities for the community in which he had made his home, and the influence of his legacy can be seen reflected in the Norwich Union of today. Norwich Union's staff have a real commitment to charitable giving. This was very much in evidence during the second world war when, with the Battle of Britain at its height, the Norwich Union Societies, the directors and staff contributed £5000 for a Spitfire to the Ministry of Aircraft Production. The aircraft, named Nuflier, was engaged on sweeps and patrols, with entries in the pilot's log book indicating trips to Lille, Cherbourg, St

Above right: *A 1914 Red Cross team from the Norwich Union Fire Office.*
Below: *'Nuflier', the Spitfire sponsored by Norwich Union pictured just before it entered service in 1941.*

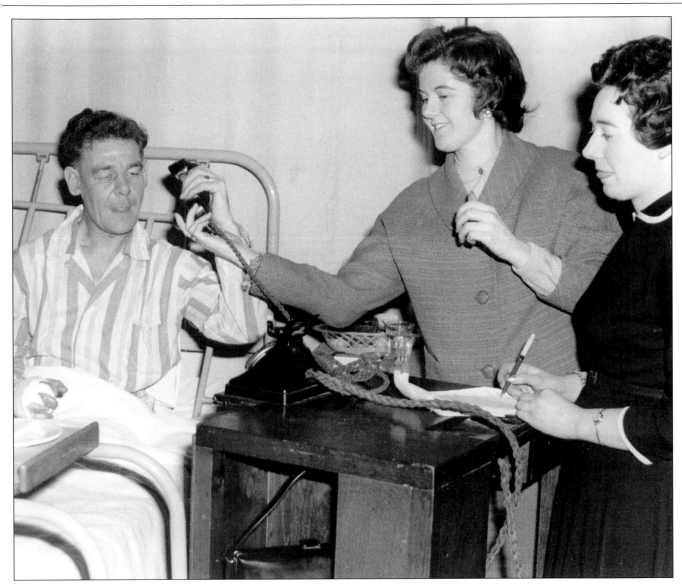

Omer, Dunkirk, Boulogne and other familiar targets. Throughout Nuflier's operational career it lived up to the traditions of the squadron with which it served. It was later transferred to the School of Army Co-operation where it was flown by pilots still in training, thus helping in the good work of bringing more pupils up to operational standard.

A charitable initiative which began after the war was the involvement of Norwich Union staff with the Norwich hospital trolley service. This scheme was organised by the Friends of Norwich Hospitals and commenced in 1956, providing patients with the facility to make private phone calls from their hospital beds. However, the facility proved so popular that it soon became obvious that one lone operator could not cope with the demand for calls; more helpers and more trolleys were needed. Mrs Sybil Burton, who was at that time the Norwich Union switchboard supervisor, managed to enrol several female staff to take on the work, and by 1958 over 100 women were taking part. Every night of the week except weekends, two women went on duty with a trolley at two Norwich hospitals,

Above: *Angela Gorrod and Joan Oliver, both of cashiers department, carry out 'telephone duty' at the West Norwich Hospital in 1959.*

while three other trolleys were manned by helpers from the GPO telephone staff at Telephone House, and thanks to their efforts many hospital patients were able to cheer themselves up by speaking to their loved ones.

Norwich Union has always taken the welfare of its own staff very seriously, and in 1963 a Head Office memorandum was circulated asking for volunteers to undergo a first aid course to supplement the existing office first aid team. Seventy Norwich Union head office staff came forward, and because of this high take-up rate two separate courses were organised, with one taking place on Tuesdays and one on Thursdays, from 4.30 pm to 6 pm. As laid down by the British Red Cross Society and the St John and St Andrew Ambulance Associations, each course consisted of six lectures, which were given by Norwich Union staff member Ralph Howell and Dr R G B Turner. Out of the 70 participants, 52 obtained certificates; and as ten members of staff had already qualified as first-aiders, this meant that the objective of having two first-aiders per floor had been achieved. Norwich Union has converted the association it had formed with St John Ambulance into a benefit for the community at large, offering free first aid training to the public. Since 1996 over 25,000 free places have been offered for first aid training.

The partnership between Norwich Union and St John Ambulance helps people learn skills that can protect and literally save lives.

There was also a tradition amongst the women members of Norwich Union head office staff of volunteering to be 'flag girls' for various charities. In the past these have included the Lynmouth Flood Relief Fund, Geranium Day (for the blind), Poppy Day, NSPCC day and several others. Like many other firms Norwich Union has acted as a 'station' where flags, credentials, tins and trays are brought and collected. Staff today continue to keep up the good work, raising thousands of pounds annually for the company's staff charity of the year, and Norwich Union generously matches the money which staff raise, pound for pound.

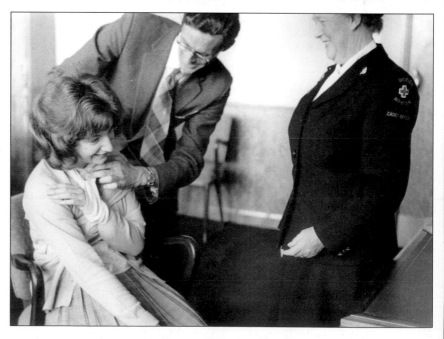

Another long-established charitable tradition is the provision of voluntary chauffeurs to take disabled people to their club meeting at the St Raphael Club. Every Wednesday night since 1958, Norwich Union staff have made themselves responsible for picking

Above: *Norwich Union employees being tested on their knowledge of the theory and practice of first aid in 1963.*
Top: *Janette Fox of Singles Department, Fire Office, beflagging a cheerful victim in St Stephens Street in 1959.*

disabled passengers up and taking them to the club for 7 pm, and for collecting them and taking them back home at the end of the evening. When this Association for the physically handicapped was begun in Norwich by Miss Margery Beattie in April 1946, it had a membership of 25 young people; since that time the Club has become an established part of Norwich community life, and its membership has grown considerably - reflected by a correspondingly rapid increase in the number of Norwich Union chauffeurs required, from 10 in 1958 to over 50 two years later!

As a major employer in the region, skills development and education are of vital importance to Norwich Union. The company places considerable emphasis on building links with schools and colleges of further education, and provides active support through teacher training days, student mentoring, work placements and careers conventions.

Another fundamental part of the company's ethos lies in building its brand and business through Corporate Community Investment. Norwich Union supports the main communities of its customers, staff and business partners through a range of community activities which includes charitable donations, community sponsorships and enterprise development in the communities close to its main offices.

Norwich Union celebrated its bicentenary in 1997. Events held to mark the occasion included a civic reception in Norwich Castle, where it was announced by the Lord Mayor of Norwich that, in recognition of the unique part that Norwich Union had played in the business and community life of Norwich since its foundation in 1797, it was to be granted the honorary freedom of the City of Norwich; and the freedom was duly conferred at a ceremony in St Andrew's Hall on 14 November 1997.

Norwich Union offers financial security to its 10 million customers worldwide. It does this by helping them save for the future, providing against the unexpected and insuring the things that are important to them. With some £58 billion of funds under management, it is one of the largest and best known UK insurers. Norwich Union aims to give its customers better protection through its wide range of good value, high performing products. Norwich Union - no one protects more.

Figures above correct at time of going to press

Below: *A photograph showing Norwich Union's presence at a careers convention at Hewett School in 1965.*

The Holden Group

A good firm to work for and better than it needs to be!

Interwar motoring was marked by clear roads, often winding and narrow but with little traffic away from major towns and popular resorts. Both people and goods chose to travel by the wonderfully reliable railway system operated by the big four companies. Lorries and vans, in the main, made local trips rather than long distance journeys.

People who had to travel to work walked, cycled or used public transport while the car owning public was in the minority. Regular deliveries to and from railway yards, shops, hotels and private houses, in many instances, were still made by horse drawn vehicles.

As a result the roads were clear for the motorist who, by and large, travelled for pleasure. Professional men such as doctors did their rounds by car, landowners, and others in isolated places, drove on business because they needed to. The number of men who drove to work was limited to the relatively few who had the money to spend for a daily luxury. Many car owners used their vehicles for holidays and outings in the summer and then laid them up, on blocks with the wheels off, in their garages for the winter. Few

WHEN in NORWICH, GARAGE at the . . .
MOST CENTRAL GARAGE IN THE CITY
Where all your motoring requirements can be supplied
THE
RELIANCE GARAGE (Nch) Ltd.
Haymarket,
Norwich
Main Dealers for Chrysler, Dodge and Renault
(any other make of Car supplied)

housewives dreamed of going to their local shops in a car while most people regarded a ride in a car as a rare treat to be savoured for many years to come.

It was in this era of the Roaring Twenties, when privileged 'Bright Young Things' aspired to sports cars in which to drive to out of town 'road house' night clubs, that the Reliance Garage first opened its doors to the motoring public. Mr H Mitchell a farmer, tired of the 'dog and stick' existence which farmers had been reduced to, with an eye to the future set up in St Stephens Square to service motor cars. The small work shop possessed an oil stove, a vice and a set of hand tools with which to deal with the innards of cars and lorries. Customers wanting to buy petrol were offered a choice between having their petrol poured from flimsy two gallon (8 litres) cans through a large funnel or taking the cans home for topping up at their convenience.

Above: An early advertisement for the Reliance Garage.
Below: A Dodge 4-5 tonner, such as was supplied and maintained by the company in its earlier days.

Next year Mr Mitchell took on young EW Holden as his apprentice fitter/mechanic. Several years later Ernest Holden had risen to be Director of the company that bears his name. By 1931 Reliance Garage leased additional and larger premises with ample parking space on the Haymarket, site of

the present C&A shop. A year later the three man staff and manager were all under the new roof while the sales side was run by one of the partners. Lorries cost £240 and new cars cost £150 when Ernest Holden earned 1/-(5p) an hour for a 54 hour week, around £120 a year in a period when many were unemployed.

In 1933, the year that saw a momentous change of government in Germany, Reliance were importing big Dodge lorries from the USA via Kew in London. These 'trucks', as the Americans called them, were shipped in pieces to be assembled in the importing country. The garage survived the precarious post depression years and grew to employ six mechanics and a salesman, who in those days wore pin-stripe or tweed suits and bow ties. 1936 saw Reliance become an approved dealer for the Longbridge based Austin Car Company and for the lovely, low slung Riley sports saloons and tourers.

In 1938 the qualified journeyman mechanic was promoted to be foreman and chargehand a year before his son was born and the world went to war again. In 1940 he became manager of Reliance Garage and soon after started to

acquire the shares which eventually brought him into control. Next year the lease ran out but it was continued for the duration of the war. The mechanics worked on lorries seven days a week and, like most civilians in 'reserved' occupations, undertook regular voluntary firewatching duties at night.

Peace, in 1945, saw Reliance move to.an old timber yard in Heigham Street where an open Dutch Barn was the only building! This problem was resolved by bricking in the sides and buying ex-Army wooden huts for £20 apiece, one of which became the paint shop. There was an acute shortage of everything in the late 1940s but then mechanics had plenty of experience in making and adapting parts which were unobtainable. This had been refined to a fine art by the

Above left: EW Holden, who took over the company in 1943. **Top:** *One of the original Chryslers supplied.* **Above right:** *A lorry that was supplied by the company in the 1960s.*

exigencies of war. Surplus military vehicles were being sold off cheaply as long as one could obtain the petrol with which to drive them away. These were adapted to civil use by staff at Reliance Garage who were proud of their self reliance!

Once petrol became de-rationed a wonderful collection of elderly cars appeared on the roads simply because wartime production had been all for military and government use.

Rather than wait years for a new model motorists, who had had vehicles requisitioned for war work, drove Bull Nose Morrises, pre-war two seaters and stately Lanchesters and other well loved British makes.

The sales department was virtually non-existent because there was little to sell but the service staff were kept busy in maintaining and repairing the historic vehicles which came their way.

The prosperous days of the 50s and 60s saw the British

car industry in full production as great names such as Alvis, Austin Riley, the independent Jowett Javelin and Singer cars returned to the roads. Reliance also sold Fords and, from 1959, became the largest Simca dealers in the country with a 10% share of the UK market. The present Chairman, Tony Holden, following an apprenticeship with Lex Service Group in London, joined his father in 1960, first working as a tester and then following an appropriate route through every department so that he was no mere 'paper qualified' manager. In 1969 Holden Motors was formed and acquired the area franchise for the Swedish Volvo marque, which signified the first big move towards the Group's current position. In 1978 the present Managing Director, Chris Carey, joined the Group with a career background of Volvo and the Lex Service Group.

A few years later in 1972 Reliance allied itself to the French Renault Dealership to sell their cars and trucks and to provide the service which has become the Holden mission statement 'to exceed customer expectations'.

Above left: The Westwick Street site when purchased... *Above right:* ...and today.
Below: An aerial view of the company's Heigham Street premises during the 1980s.

At this time a new Group bodyshop was developed on a two acre site in Whiffler Road which takes responsibility for all the marques within the Group and all types. Other trading partnerships were entered into with overseas manufacturers, namely, in 1982, the Swedish car and aircraft company Saab which also makes rather splendid cars. Next in 1993 the Detroit giant Chrysler was once more re-associated with the Group with the highly popular Jeep and Chrysler range. This was followed by Honda in 1995, and Mitsubishi in 1996.

Today the Companies of the Holden Group serve the populations of Norfolk and Suffolk in a rural area where reputation is all important. In this company the can is carried all the way to the top, indeed the management team walk around the shop floor to pick it up. The art of leading well is one which at Holdens is fostered at all levels, which is to be expected when following in the footsteps of a founder who worked his way up through every position. Holden managers are expected to be experts capable of demonstrating their skills to staff who appreciate coaching 'the Holden way'. Every one of the team of 211 are responsible for the reputation of their firm in the eyes of their customers who talk to their acquaintances and friends about the service they receive.

Holden's play a responsible and neighbourly part in the life of their locality in a number of ways. The training given by St John's Ambulance Brigade to the group's First Aiders is recognised by practical support for the nursing charity. At another level Holdens supported the Young Entrepreneurs from Norwich High School in a year long enterprise in which they learned to set up and run a company which produced goods for sale. The company sensibly encourages staff to participate in voluntary work for a variety of their own community organisations as this enriches their characters and widens their experience and understanding of the people the firm deals with. Work experience for teenagers is the norm today and, while some companies use unwelcome youngsters as cheap labour, Holdens aim at providing a worthwhile training experience to show boys and girls just how satisfying a career in the motor industry can be. The Company now enjoys a turnover in excess of £70 million per annum and is in the top 100 motor groups in the UK.

Above left: *Holden Motors gained Investors in People status in 1995.*
Top: *One of the company's many dealerships.*

There's been a rush in this shop since 1864

It is simply not possible to walk past the corner of Norwich's Bridewell Alley and Bedford Street without being tempted to stop for a closer look at the attractive selection of baskets and wickerwork on display outside Hovells' doorway, which in turn will lead, time permitting, to a happy hour or so exploring the 'labyrinth of surprises' inside. The nine floor levels are packed with a tremendous range of exciting gifts from all around the world, together with a large selection of well-crafted pine and cane furniture and other pleasing items. Baskets are still stocked, too, in a large array of shapes and sizes. As we admire the craftsmanship which has gone into their making, it is appropriate to think back to the long tradition of cottage industry on this site.

The long weavers' window on the top floor is an indication that handicraft weavers worked here in the 17th and 18th centuries, weaving on their looms the fine worsted and silken cloths which were a staple part of the city's trade. In 1799 David Soman, an emigrant from the French revolution, bought the building and made fur caps there. As the boot and shoe trade took over locally from the old weaving industry, Soman began making footwear instead of headwear; he also became a leather merchant, and in the 1840s he went into partnership with his son-in-law Philip Haldinstein to found the major shoe manufacturer Bally's of Norwich, and moved to bigger premises.

It was at this point, in 1864, that the shop became the home of W B Hovell. W B Hovell, like his father before him, was a basket-maker. There was tremendous demand for wickerwork in Norwich at that time. Fishermen needed crab pots, lobster pots, herring

swills and various other specialist items, farmers needed skeps and wicker hurdles, tradesmen needed delivery baskets and hampers, and housewives needed shopping baskets and laundry baskets. Many people slept on rush mattresses as it was widely believed that rushes kept the vermin away; for the same reason, farm labourers carried their dinner to the fields in frail-baskets which were made of rushes. And there was also a market for wicker furniture, which had become fashionable. W B Hovell was well-known for his high standard of craftsmanship, and his shop prospered; his son William Edward also came into the business, and by 1881 over twenty highly-skilled craftsmen were employed, several of whom were colourful characters. The basket-makers worked on the first floor of the building, and the chair-makers worked on the second floor. William Hovell owned three acres of land at Old Lakenham, which provided most of the osiers used by Hovells' workers, but sometimes it was necessary to buy in extra supplies. Men would then go to one of the Norfolk estates to cut the willow, and bring it back by horse and cart and by wherry.

Basket-making was traditionally man's work, and the shop was very badly affected when its workers were called up for service during the first world war. W E Hovell's two sons joined the army, and sadly both were killed; only one of the old basket-makers came back from the war to resume his craft. Business was made even more difficult by the introduction of free trade, with cheap imported baskets being sold, sometimes for less than the cost of manufacture. In the period between the wars very few baskets were made at Hovells; instead, W E Hovell, who was joined in 1918 by his daughter Miss D K Hovell, was forced to rely to an increasing extent on selling imported goods. William carried on working until his death in 1958, at the age of 91, and from 1958 until 1969 the shop was run by Miss Hovell. who built up a wide selection of wicker and canework, both imported and from the leading manufacturers in this country. Meanwhile the Hovell family continued to reside above the shop until the mid 60s.

In 1969 Miss Hovell sold the shop to the Butcher family, with the stipulation that the name of Hovells should be kept, and began a well-earned retirement. The Butcher family, themselves the proprietors of the long-established family drapery business in Swan Lane, survived disaster in November 1978 when a fire occurred at Hovell's premises; fortunately damage was kept to a minimum, and within a few days Hovells was able to reopen the ground floor for business. During rebuilding, every effort was made to preserve the original facade, and although some alteration to the Bedford Street side proved inevitable, the 17th century style of the building has been successfully preserved, and Hovells, with its traditional range of baskets, wickerwork, cane and pine, remains one of the well-loved features of this picturesque and historic area of the city.

Above and facing page: *Hovells at the turn of the century.*

Family values bring material success

The Butcher family has been looking after the drapery needs of Norwich for almost a century, since the establishment of the business in King Street in 1905. G F Butcher, who was responsible for starting the firm, had been manager of Moores the Drapers in St Benedicts, Norwich. Three years later the business moved to new premises at Norfolk House, Bedford Street, Norwich, where Mr Butcher took over the well-established drapery emporium of George Diggens & Co. Here he was joined in due course by his three sons, after they had trained at Shinners of Sutton, London. Today, Butchers is well known for its extensive range of soft furnishings, particularly carpets, curtains and bedding, as well as its very large interior design department offering thousands of furnishing variations.

In the early days cotton and linen were the basic materials of the drapery trade, and G F Butcher's reputation for trading in high quality items which gave good service soon spread. They stocked an excellent range of goods which attracted customers from all over the area. World War I provided the family firm with its first serious challenge; some products were simply not available, and others were difficult to obtain, but the firm had by that time established good contacts in the trade and it managed to survive, and in the period between the wars it was able to build up the range of goods it supplied.

By the mid 1930s new fabrics were becoming available with the development of synthetic fibres, and G F Butcher's 1937 Great Sale included Winceyette nightdresses, still quite expensive at three shillings and eightpence ha'penny or four shillings and eightpence ha'penny each (about 18p or

Above: An early reciept.
Below: Geo Diggens' premises.

sale. Towels came in white or colours, and reversible wool rugs were available in plain fawn, green, rose or blue. All-wool 'Witney' blankets with blue borders were beautifully soft and warm but represented a serious investment at 29/11 (£1.50) for extra large; however, a single mattress would set you back less than fifteen bob, while even a double mattress could be had for less than a pound. There was no King Size in those days!

Difficult trading conditions returned in the second world war, although the Utility Scheme which was introduced in 1941 helped regulate the situation. Since then, the Butcher family has built the business up steadily in the face of keen competition from the multiples and other local stores, keeping the emphasis on customer care and good value and stocking quality goods to suit all generations of customers in Norwich, Norfolk and Suffolk. The slogan 'You Can Get It At Butchers' is no idle boast; Butchers has a remarkably extensive range of drapery and haberdashery items, and prides itself on being able match the requirements of even the most demanding customers.

23p) as compared to woven nightdresses at one and elevenpence ha'penny (just under 10p). Combinations in interlock or striped silk were also priced at one and elevenpence ha'penny a pair, wool vests and opera tops cost a shilling each (5p), and ladies' art silk knickers cost a shilling or one and threepence (5p or 6p). Household linen was still predominately white or unbleached, with 'Dorma' white cotton blankets priced from two shillings (10p) to four shillings (20p) depending on size, and 'Dorma' unbleached sheets for four and sixpence ha'penny (23p) for the smallest size to seven and six (38p) for the largest. 'Dorcas' pure white sheets were more expensive, with a pair of large size hemstiched sheets priced at nine and elevenpence (50p) a pair, but they had a reputation for lasting longer. Pillowcases were available in white, hemstitched, or hemstitched and scalloped; feather pillows were reduced from half a crown (13p) to a florin (10p) for the Great Sale, and bags of purified feathers for pillows and cushions were available at ninepence three farthings (5p) per bag. Curtain nets came in the popular Biscuit shade, and patterned cretonne was sixpence a yard in the

Today, Butchers is still a family firm, with John Butcher as Chairman and Jonathan and James Butcher as Joint Managing Directors. Jonathan and James are the fourth generation to run the business - while Mr Harold Butcher, one of the original directors, still attends on a regular basis at the age of 94.

In 1969 the Butcher family became the proprietors of another long-established Norwich family business when the time came for Miss Hovell, of the nearby Hovell's store on the corner of Bridewell Alley, to retire. Having run Hovell's basket shop single-handed for many years, she elected to sell it to the Butchers, knowing that this would ensure that the family values of the business would be preserved. Butchers have continued to run the basket shop in the traditional way, retaining Hovell's name as Miss Hovell wished, and the continuing success of both these businesses is proof that genuine family commitment to providing quality goods and service will always be appreciated by the people of Norwich and the surrounding area.

Above: *An advertisement dating from the 1950s.*

A brush with heritage and technology

Brushmaking is thought to be one of the oldest crafts in the world. We know from cave paintings that cavemen were making and using brushes some 16,000 years ago. In Norfolk, this traditional craft can be traced back a mere three centuries.

There is evidence that by the early 18th century there were numerous small brushmaking workshops throughout Norfolk. Amongst them was the Norwich company SD Page & Sons which began business in 1746 from the Haymarket in the centre of the city. Over the years S D Page & Sons moved from Norwich to Wymondham, changed its name to the Briton Brush Company then Briton Chadwick then Acorn Decorating Products. In 1990 it merged with the Hamilton Group, which Charles Foster Hamilton had set up in 1811 in Brick Lane, London. Then, in 1996, Hamilton Acorn became a private company once again following a Management Buy-Out. It was purchased by three of its Directors and Close Investment Management Ltd.

Hamilton Acorn's continuing reputation for making superior brushes is based on more than 250 years of experience. The Hamilton Acorn factory now based in Attleborough produces some 10 million paintbrushes and 2 1/2 million paint rollers a year. Specialist brushes are still made by hand using traditional skills but this is backed up with some of the most modern equipment in the world.

Every decorator whether professional or DIY, knows that the quality of the finish is entirely dependent upon the brush used. The Hamilton brand name is considered in the professional trade to indicate the best brushes in the world and they are used by professional decorators to achieve the finest finish.For DIY enthusiasts who may not have the professional's skill, the innovative technology of the Acorn range of painting products helps overcome the users' lack of skill and ensure the DIYer achieves a first class result.

When Hamilton Acorn's business began all those years ago, hog bristles would have been used in many of its brushes, as would hairs such as hare, sable and squirrel. But in more recent times the practice of breeding hogs for their meat rather than for their bristles has resulted in a serious shortage of supplies. Paintbrush manufacturers have therefore had to look for alternatives and synthetic filaments have been developed to take the place of bristle.

Above left: *Samuel Deyns (1720 - 1806), founder of SD Page & Sons.* ***Above right:*** *A show case merchandiser for one of the Briton ranges circa 1930.* ***Below:*** *The premises in the early 1900s.*

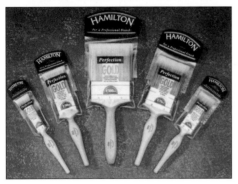

Early synthetic filaments were found to be poor substitutes for natural bristle, but Hamilton Acorn has managed to match the performance of natural bristle, and in many cases beat it, with an advanced synthetic fibre called Bristolon. Many synthetic fibres fail to hold the paint because they have smooth surfaces which the paint simply runs off. Hamilton Acorn in its quest for technical excellence, identified Bristolon as the best substitute because, just like natural bristle, it has a rough surface texture resembling tree bark, produced by a patented extrusion process. This produces better paint pick-up and allows controlled delivery of the paint onto the surface and is unique to Hamilton Acorn in the UK.

Synthetic filament brushes now account for a significant and increasing percentage of the company's production. And not content to merely maintain the traditional high performance level of its products, Hamilton Acorn has actually been able to derive added benefits from the use of synthetic filaments. Precise specifications for particular functions can be achieved by careful blending of filaments of different lengths and using a mixture of polyester and nylon, so the customer can be sure of the right product for every type of job, every type of coating and every type of surface. Also by controlling the formulations, identical levels of performance can be achieved every time - something which is simply not possible with natural bristle.

As the brushmaking industry has had to adapt to these changes, Hamilton Acorn's policy of continuous product development has confirmed its position as a leader in its field. A programme of investment in production equipment and methods and a dedicated Technical Services Laboratory have led to state of the art manufacturing facilities and a range of products which outperform those of competitors. The company was the first UK manufacturer of paint applicators to be awarded ISO 9002 and in 1994 it won the Arthur Andersen/Management Today Best Practice Awards for Service Excellence within the region. This business excellence was reinforced recently when the company won the Barclays Business of the Year Award and the Norwich & Peterborough Customer Care Award at the EDP Business Awards in 1998.

In more than two and a half centuries of brush making, Hamilton Acorn has been fortunate in enjoying the services of many notable craftsmen and innovators committed to traditional values. By pursuing its quest for excellence through today's technology, the company will continue to uphold these values well into the next millennium.

Above: Hamilton Acorn's Head Office at Halford Road, Attleborough.
Left: Some of the more recent developments.
Below: The buy-out team. From left to right: Shirley Henderson, Dennis Marrison and Ralph Brindle.

Dogs, collars, chucks, worms and vices

Readers who have visited the Bridewell Museum in Norwich recently may well have been intrigued by the stand devoted to Edward Hines Engineers, with its fascinating display of early lathes and machinery and its photographic record of an era before mass-production, when manufacturers took great pride in their work, when each piece of machinery was individually crafted, when quality was the byword and when customers expected and got personal attention from their suppliers and made a practice of writing to express their opinion of the goods they had received.

The firm of Edward Hines Engineers Limited was founded in 1820 at the Griffin Engineering Works, St Margarets. Its founder Edward Hines was a member of the Institute of Mechanical Engineers, as was his son Charles Edward, to whom the firm passed after his father's death - although Charles Edward was clearly a man of many parts; an entry in the 1859 edition of Rogers Directory of Norwich and Neighbourhood lists him as "HINES, Charles, engineer, lathe and tool maker, ivory, hardwood, and metal turner, machinist and agent to the Briton Life Association, Muspole Street, St George's'. After Charles' death the firm stayed in the family for another three generations before being sold by the brothers, Edward and Geoffrey Hines in 1969 to Richard Payne of Thurne Engineering, subsequently moving to premises in Oak Street and then St Mary's Works, Duke Street, where it is located today.

The firm of Edward Hines held patents for many lathes and other tools. The literature which the firm distributed (printed, in one instance at least, by Pentney and Co. at the 'Northumbrian' Steam Printing Works, St Benedict's, Norwich) is very informative, not only about the products themselves and the general engineering principles upon which they are based, but also about the company itself. For instance, in a leaflet produced in the late 19th century, entitled 'The Face Plate - A Universal Chuck', Mr Hines begins by explaining that the name 'chuck' derives from the expression sometimes used by workmen when deciding how to attach work in hand to the machinery - 'chuck it on'! He then describes in some detail the process of chucking, with useful hints on how to get the best results,

common pitfalls to avoid, and advice on the best design for a chuck: 'The diagram herewith illustrates a most excellent design for a Face Plate Chuck, and is the pattern in general use throughout my own workshops,' Mr Hines tells us, helpfully going on to explain the manufacturing process in case the reader prefers to make his own. Advertising was rather more subtle in those days: 'We have supplied some of these fittings . . . with the utmost satisfaction,' he says modestly, going on to bemoan that 'other firms have imitated them in a rough fashion, and some vile things are in the market', while in another brochure he warns that 'It is well known that where cheapness is the principal feature, excellence is most likely to be sacrificed'.

As well as making tools for serious manufacturers and 'practical workers', Mr Hines also patented a range of turning lathes and machine tools for amateurs - coping with stress is clearly not a new problem, as more than a century ago Mr Hines was promoting turning as a relaxation therapy! 'Noblemen, clergymen and professional gentlemen, have for a considerable period of time sought relaxation from mental and physical

Above: Edward Hines' concern for quality has been rewarded with many prizes and medals for excellence of workmanship over the years, and the originals of these can be seen at the Bridewell Museum, Norwich where a section has been devoted to the Hines Firm. **Top:** *An early advertisement for the 'Universal Cutter Bar'.* **Below:** *Edward Sidney Hines (second left) and Sidney Harry Hines (centre) outside the premises in the early 1900s.*

elevators; one post-war catalogue of their light precision engineering products illustrates a selection of chocolate machinery such as chocolate piping machines and Easter Egg spinning machines, again with the emphasis on their ability to meet customers' exact requirements.

Today, Edward Hines (Engineers) Ltd is one of the largest sub-contract engineering companies in East Anglia. Its machine shop is equipped with a combination of the latest CNC (Computer Numeric Controlled) mills and CNC lathes, plus some older but highly

strain in the agreeable recreation of turning, which is not only a pleasant but useful pastime', and worried business men could 'unbend their minds, and relax their energies in producing some fancy or useful article as a present to their family or friends.' A Student's Outfit, comprising a 4" centre lathe, could be had for 18 guineas, or the more ambitious could invest in a 4'6" Officer's Combination Lathe for 65 guineas. The company received a great deal of complimentary feedback from satisfied customers, with many comments to the effect of: 'I am greatly pleased with the Cutter Bar you sent me, it works beautifully', and the occasional rather more cryptic comment such as, 'You will be glad to know that the Lathe improves on acquaintance.' From inventing, patenting and manufacturing a comprehensive range of lathes, chucks, cutter bars and related tools and accessories such as boring collars, clamping dogs, worms and vices, Edward Hines diversified somewhat into sanding machines, saw benches, chutes, conveyors and

productive machines such as an Elgamill with a 6-metre bed which has been upgraded with the latest CNC unit. The sheet-metal department specialises in the fabrication of stainless steel components and assemblies from sheets which are cut, punched, folded and welded to produce the finished articles which often include machined components. These products are then supplied to the manufactures of equipment for a diverse range of markets which include food and chemical processing and the off-shore oil, automotive, scientific and defence industries. The common thread is quality with hygiene requirements or corrosion resistance.

In addition, the Company has an active resale operation from their Engineering Stores which includes a trade counter and local delivery service The range of product lines offered includes; power transmissions (chains and sprockets, V-belts and pulleys, timing belts and taper-lock pulleys, flat-belt drives, couplings, gears and gear boxes, motors and controllers); pneumatics (cylinders and actuators, valves, solenoids, timers, flow regulators, push-in and compression fittings, filters and tubing); plus others such as lifting tackle and specialised lubricants. As well as supplying a large range of standard items 'off-the-shelf', the Company specialises in modifying those standard items to solve non-standard problems.

In all areas, quality remains an essential part of the Company's service to its customers. This quality still includes consistent high standards of manufacture, maintenance of delivery promises and personal attention, all included in the Company's current ISO 9002 Certification.

Above: *Sidney Harry Hines looking at a model traction engine designed by Edward Hines Engineers.* ***Left:*** *The premises in the late 1970s.*

Slippers made to last

Slippers and shoes have been made in Norwich since the Middle Ages. Until the introduction of machinery in the later nineteenth century every one from ploughmen to peers wore hand made footwear. Many of the earlier styles were inter-changeable from one foot to another until broken in to left or right foot, probably at some discomfort to the feet. Shoes were, and are, made from a variety of leathers and cloths to suit the needs of the wearers. During the early seventeenth century Catholic France lost many thousands of her finest craftsmen, Protestants all, who fled the persecution of the Dragonards. These refugees settled in England, and other Protestant lands, which they enriched by their fine workmanship in different crafts including leather work and shoe making.

Hand made shoes have been sold from shops, in London Street, with family links to the Bowhills since 1843. One of the fore-runners of the present firm was the Cordwainer (leather worker) Robert Wright working from premises near the former Red Lion Inn. By 1859 he was in partnership making boots, which came above the calf, and shoes, which then came above the ankle,

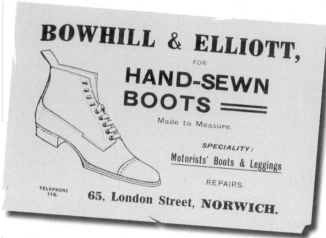

with a Mr Base. At the same time Obadiah Henry Bowhill who was making shoes in Pottergate, not far from the Cathedral, was beginning to take an interest in the older business, which he purchased in 1874.

Above: *An advertisement from 1916.*
Below: *A late 1940s view of the firm's premises in London Street, Norwich.*

Two of his four sons entered into business with him while his daughter Agnes married Thomas Baines Elliott when both were employed by a local silk mercer. Obadiah Bowhill sold his business in 1894 to son Obadiah Herbert Bowhill and son-in-law TB Elliott to run between them for the benefit of the two families. They built on his foundation of making footwear for county and clergy, professional, business and farming families all with special requirements for outdoor and indoor use. Such a variety of clientele enabled them to provide for both the elders, who wanted what they were used to, and the young entry who preferred something with a bit of dash about it.

The turn of the century saw the firm making quantities of bespoke riding boots for both cavalry and infantry officers, who supplied their own chargers and kit, from the local garrison. During the South African War, in which many infantry units were transformed into mounted infantry to cope with the mounted Boer Commandoes, Bowhill and Elliott supplied the ankle boots and both cloth puttees and the farmers' style leather gaiters which superseded long boots for military wear. As long as farmers and their horsemen wore breeches there was a trade for leather gaiters which lasted until the 1950s in some areas.

Many young men who had shoes made before leaving home to make their way in the colonies ordered their military boots from Bowhill and Elliott on the outbreak of war in 1914. This was a simple matter as all good

bootmakers kept their customers' lasts as long as they lived! Following the return to peacetime trading after the Great War the firm continued to make shoes to order even supplying pupils at Norwich Grammar and Suffield Park schools. Having overcome the Depression the family were able to deal with the military demands of World War II, indeed it was these that kept business going in the difficult days of rationing of all materials with any military value.

Today Bowhill and Elliott combine the pleasures of bespoke wear with traditional skills and the best of materials so that one is hardly aware of wearing their products. Such products give immense satisfaction to the craftsmen and women who make them, a joy which is shared by the sales staff who handle them and by the customers whose feet and carriage benefit from the ultimate in comfort.

The deliciously comfortable hand turned slippers are made by the associated O-So-Easie Slipper Company founded by Jack Hale in 1939. This originated in the former Enterprise Picture house and was carried on, after his death by the redoubtable Mrs Hale until 1960 when Bowhill and Elliott bought the business. Their slippers are hand made inside out and then carefully pulled out to their proper shape for use in bedroom, court or evening wear.

Above: A craftsman using traditional tools and skills to produce quality footwear.

Buildings and Funerals

GW Gooch worked for Robert Bayes, Carpenter & Undertaker, who had established his business in the mid-nineteenth century in Oxford Street, Norwich. Death was then a frequent visitor to families of all classes. One of the major reasons why the Victorians bred so prolifically was to ensure that there were sufficient descendants to keep the family going or to care for aged parents. The Victorian way of death was brought about partly by public sanitation totally inadequate for the needs of a burgeoning urban population and partly by the state of medical knowledge where military horses were watered above stream from men collecting drinking water. It was embellished by the need felt by all classes to appear respectable, even in death, by putting on the best show affordable to impress neighbours.

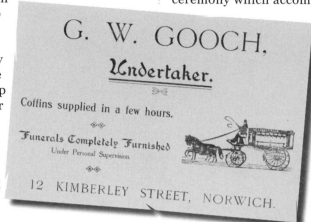

G. W. GOOCH,
Undertaker.

Coffins supplied in a few hours.

Funerals Completely Furnished
Under Personal Supervision.

12 KIMBERLEY STREET, NORWICH.

Above: An early advertisement for the firm.
Below: The management and staff in the early 1900s.

Undertakers such as Robert Bayes, joined by young Garrard William Gooch in 1898, catered splendidly for this fascination with death and the all important ceremony which accompanied the deceased on their last earthly journey. The simple hand cart biers common to rural churches were superseded by magnificent black hearses ornamented with engraved glass panels, gold leaf and black feathers drawn by shining black horses. Paupers may have had the simplest and socially shaming funerals but the better off shelled out for black banners and hired 'weepers' veiled in black to follow in a procession of public grief. It was then a good business for small local firms to trade in.

When Mr Bayes retired in 1912 he sold the thriving Kimberley Street business to Mr G W Gooch where the firm continues to this day. During this period it was common for undertakers to divide their work between the allied fields of organising funerals for

the benefit of the bereaved, making coffins and doing contract joinery and carpentry for builders and householders.

GW Gooch was joined by his sons Sydney James and Edward George to undertake the myriad responsibilities of such a varied occupation.

During the trying days of two world wars when the raw materials of these allied trades were in short supply and strictly rationed the firm operated short-handed as men were called up either into the forces of the Crown or into essential war work in other industries. As more men met their deaths away from home there was a reduced trade to cater for.

For three generations the Gooch family have worked as builders-cum-undertakers to build up a reputation where temperament and attitude in dealing with clients have been of prime importance. The craftmanship and organisational expertise of funeral directors must be backed by kindness and understanding towards the bereaved who rely on their professionalism to reduce the suffering of those left behind. As people can die at work or in public places as readily as when in hospitals or in their own homes the services of GW Gooch & Sons are as often called upon by hospitals and local authorities as by families and individuals. The quality and customer care rendered in a funeral is remembered, like a wedding,

long after the event. The Big G of GW Gooch & Sons is a well known Norwich trade mark which spells reliability to all who need the reassurance which comes from dealing with a small family business.

As builders, which is the main business of GW Gooch & Sons, they have built up an enviable reputation in the changing world. Having worked in the fine city of Norwich and surrounding area for well over one and a half centuries, they have contributed to many fine construction projects ranging from alterations to hospitals, new churches and schools to name but a few and above all, the conservation and preservation of many historical buildings which are the showpiece of the fine city of Norwich and Norfolk.

Building awards won include the European Architectural Heritage Year Award for for the Balderston Court project, Good Design in Housing 1975 and a Civic Trust Award, 1972 for the restoration work carried out in Sussex Street and St Augustine's Street.

The company today is under the directorship of the founder's grandson, Edward GF Gooch, and his fellow director, DH Hoy and continues to produce the skills and craftmanship which it has gained from the knowledge of over one and a half centuries in business.

Above: *A horse-drawn hearse at the turn of the 20th century.*

Still making an impression after four generations - est 1840

In 1887 a commercial property in Aylsham came up for sale - a former Post Office which had been turned into a stationery shop with a printing works above. It was bought by Charles Henry Barnwell, a printer from Hull and thus continued a family business which has remained in Aylsham and in the hands of the Barnwells ever since.

Charles married a local lady from Hull, she looked after the shop while he organised the printing. Mrs. Barnwell proved a good business lady and negotiated some shrewd property deals. The couple were able to hand on a thriving concern to their son Frederick Charles; he, like his father, concentrated on running the print works, while his wife's sister Winnie managed the shop until she was well into her 70's. Winnie is 97 at the time of writing.

Frederick was strictly a Letterpress printer, with hand-fed machines. Working hours were 8.00 a.m. to 5.30 p.m. on weekdays and 8.00 to 12 noon on Saturdays. Barnwell's issued invoices every quarter, and prices remained identical from one quarter to the next - life was much simpler before inflation!

Fathers were more autocratic then too; when Frederick's 15 year old son Michael started work in 1952, he was given responsibility for delivering newspapers, folding the advertisement sheets which the firm printed for the Church magazine, and little else; his father was in no hurry to let his son in on the secrets of the trade. Consequently when Frederick suffered a stroke at work at the age of 79, Michael was scarcely ready to take over the business.

Michael set about re-organising the business and implemented many changes, beginning with a thorough clearout, which uncovered so much dust he got asthma. Nothing daunted, he took tablets for his asthma, sold a lot of old magazines and Presses to make room for new equipment, and then purchased a Letterpress Platen. As it was clear that litho printing was on its way in, he also invested in an A3 Litho press, and soon the firm was producing high-quality printing. He also undertook his own binding, previously done in Norwich. His wife Linda, whom he married in 1966, took over this operation. She did collating from home and the finishing at Aylsham. All this was done whilst bringing up two small boys, and without payment, thus helping to build the family business. Michael also seconded his mother to help Linda when time was short. On one occasion Michael recalls taking his family out for a drive while his wife Linda folded a rush job in the car. Room quickly ran out, first the shop was expanded, then in 1979 he

SILVER JUBILEE
1935

F. C. BARNWELL
Market Place AYLSHAM Norfolk

Above left: *Frederick Charles Barnwell.*
Above right: *An advertisement by the company, offering their printing services for the Silver Jubilee of 1935.*
Below left: *An early view of Market Place, Aylsham during the coronation of Queen Elizabeth II.* ***Below right:*** *The company moved premises to Penfold Street in the late 1970s. A wall had to be taken down in order to move the machines.*

purchased the old Cooperative building just around the corner. This was to be the new home of the printing works.

For most of his working life Michael Barnwell worked a seven day week, spending Sunday doing invoices and quotes. A hard worker himself he kept an eagle eye on his staff's timekeeping and expected them to make time up when they were late. To save money in the early days he would buy printing equipment out of Exchange & Mart, and one year he even took the gamble of not paying the buildings insurance for a year to raise capital. However it is fortunate that he only took this drastic measure once, because one cold frosty night in 1982 when Michael and a colleague were working late, an old boiler overheated and set fire to the roof. Sparks from the roof set fire to the paper on the floor, and although the fire brigade arrived within minutes a considerable amount of damage was done. Undaunted, Michael hired a trailer and with his staff his wife and his two sons, Julian and Lincoln cleared out the premises. Such were their efforts and those of the fire brigade, the printing works was up and running in a matter of days. Julian joined the business at the age of 16. Remembering his own apprenticeship, Michael started him off stitching draw tickets and running a small roto-print press. Having finished college and his apprenticeship, Julian moved to Brighton. Armed with his City & Guilds Certificate he started work there as a printer. He used this time to learn new skills, ideas and working methods. He then travelled Australia for a few months, before returning to Aylsham. On leaving school, Lincoln joined his father and brother. His apprenticeship was spent on the presses, he also finished his time having achieved his City & Guilds.

In 1994 Julian and Lincoln took over the business from Michael, who, not wishing to retire completely, took a part time role in charge of sales and deliveries. Another new generation at the helm evoked more new ideas and investment throughout the factory; new presses, new bindery equipment, more staff and more work. Once again space was scarce; this led to what would turn out to be a two year expansion programme.

Derelict property adjacent to the printing works was purchased from the neighbouring Black Boys Public House. Building industrial premises in the middle of a town, let alone a conservation area was to be no simple task. However, after working closely with both the planning and conservation departments the local council agreed to the erection of a two storey building, that would not only double the size of the printing works but would also add to and compliment the character of the town itself. Such was the success of the completed building, it received an Enhancement Award from the District Council.

The new building was going to be in part home of the pre-press department. This was about to undertake the biggest single change Barnwell Printers had seen. Digital technology was upon them. The investment in this technology meant that Barnwells became completely self-sufficient for all its pre-press needs, thus meeting the increasing demand for faster turnaround times and the ability for customers to see jobs immediately with the increased workflow came the need for even faster, larger presses.

Today Barnwells is committed to continue its investment in new technology and equipment to enable it to go on producing quality work, with fast turn around times. Investment in machinery alone is not enough investment in people has also always been important. It is not just the business of four generations but also the loyalty, dedication and skills of all of their employees that ensures the future of Barnwells.

Above: *The new building taking shape.*
Below: *Work completed, 1998.*

The city's best loved china shop

The early history of Loose of Norwich has unfortunately been somewhat obscured by the passing of time, but one thing is certain: it is a very old-established business, dating back, as far as can be ascertained from Trade Directories of the time, to 1791. It is believed that there is a connection through marriage between the Loose family and the Stevens family, and certainly both families have traded in Norwich for at least two centuries, with men of those names being listed, at various times and at various addresses, as 'hat-maker and furniture broker', 'grocer and tallow chandler; cabinet maker', 'housebroker', and 'china, glass and earthenware dealer'.

We do know, however, that at the beginning of the 20th century a successful china, glass and earthenware business in Magdalen Street was being run by Jimmy Loose. When Jimmy retired at the age of 55 in 1912, two years after the death of his wife, the business was taken over by his daughter Leila and son-in-law Robbie Ruymp. Miss Leila, as she liked to be called, managed the staff, and did so fairly but strictly, having all her shop girls dress in black, deducting a penny a week from their wages for a 'breakages' fund and carrying out staff training classes at the back of the shop to show the girls to serve a customer. Girls would be employed from the age of fourteen, and would begin at the front of the shop - the draughtiest position, with baskets of odd, chipped white cups and earthenware jugs for sale at

Above: *One of Loose's lorries in the 1930s.*
Below: *Staff dressed as Wedgwood Portland vases during the Norfolk & Norwich Carnival in July 1931.*

1d each - from where they hoped to be promoted to the more expensive goods further into the shop and possibly even to the glass showroom on the first floor.

Robbie ran the business, in a rather idiosyncratic way and with painstaking attention to detail, from an office which overlooked the main shop; having survived the first world war, the business began to expand. A number of former shop assistants and warehousemen who worked for Loose's in the 1920s and 30s responded to an appeal in the Eastern Evening News in 1989 for information on Loose's early days, and all of them seem to have happy memories of a busy, friendly, hardworking firm, where a high standard of professionalism was expected but where the annual staff outing to the seaside and the annual Sports Days were enthusiastically enjoyed by owners and employees alike. Jimmy Loose, retired and living at Great Yarmouth, still paid regular visits to the shop, and is remembered with affection as a great character. He took a particular interest in a magnificent vine which grew in a glass-roofed arcade where china and glass was displayed, and would distribute the bunches of grapes it produced, giving some to customers and staff but taking most to the Norfolk and Norwich Hospital

Business suffered during the depression, but with its diverse lines, from the cheapest to the most expensive, it managed to survive. At around this time Gerald Brett, whose father had a furniture retailing business in St Benedict's Street, was keen to start his own business, Robbie and Leila Ruymp, who had no children, were thinking of retiring, and a deal was

struck. Gerald Brett became the new proprietor of Loose's in 1938. Gerald ran things in quite a different way from the Ruymps, having a much more relaxed style - he also changed the staff uniform from black to green-and-cream. But on June 27 1942 disaster struck when the shop was set ablaze during a bombing raid; stock was destroyed and the premises were left uninhabitable. Somehow Gerald and his staff managed to sort out the mess, get hold of new stock from the suppliers and open a temporary shop further along Magdalen Street; then Gerald was called up into the Navy. He returned after the war to find his business thriving as well as could be expected under the circumstances, and resolved to re-develop the original site, although his first applications to the authorities for permission to do this were refused on the grounds that building materials were in short supply. In the meanwhile he was able to buy the temporary premises at No. 43, and in the course of this transaction it transpired among the previous owners of No. 43 was a certain Jimmy Loose! Gerald eventually triumphed in his fight to obtain planning permission.

As Loose's Ltd looks forward to its third centenary, the Company and staff are prepared for increased competition and are aware of how rapidly their market place is changing. The company believes that a professionally run specialist family business can continue to flourish by their individuality and service - being the best loved specialist shop for tableware and giftware.

Above: *The company's premises in 1951.*

They 'managed' in 1919 - but in 1999 they 'manage' even better

The Honingham building firm of H Smith and Sons has been very much a family business for 80 years. Established in 1919 by Herbert Smith, it was carried on by his two sons Herbert Alfred (Bert) and George between 1958 and 1970, and is now run by George's two sons, John and Alan.

In terms of work, the company has come a long way in those 80 years. Now specialising in prestigious contracts for local education authorities, housing associations, nursing homes and private individuals, the firm began by carrying out small works, and occasionally building a house or two. Herbert had set up in business in a small garage in Honingham, near Norwich, after a varied career which had included being an errand boy - a position from which he was sacked for wishing a customer 'compliments of the season' instead of asking her for a tip; assisting in an iron foundry - where he made the mistake of handing a smelter a ladle with a few drops of water and was dismissed again; and working as an estate carpenter at Honingham Estate. During the first world war he was employed by Mann Egerton, building aeroplanes, and when this war work ended Herbert, with £50 to his name and a wife and four children to support, discovered that his former position at Honingham Estate had been filled. Bravely, he started his own business; Lord Aylwyn put £50 at his disposal, should he need it, but at the end of a year the money was

untouched and Herbert was able to politely thank Lord Aylwyn and say, 'We have managed.'

Herbert's son Bert started working full-time in 1922, and George joined as a bricklayer's apprentice some ten years later. A building site in those days was the scene of intensive manual labour; not only was excavation work a manual job, but concrete was mixed by hand - brick rubble was broken up manually for the aggregate, ten-stone sacks of lump lime for the mortar were slaked in tanks of water and stirred, then pailed out of the tank, sieved into a ring of sand and finally mixed by hand into mortar. Then, if it was to be used for plastering, cow hair was added, having first been beaten to remove all the knots before being soaked in a pail of water, carefully parted and mixed. Today's building apprentices would stare in amazement at these processes; however, George believes that buildings constructed then withstood movement better than many modern day structures, which need many more expansion joints to absorb movement.

Twenty-one year old George was called up on 1st December 1939, and served initially in France, then in the Middle East

Above: A company letterhead dating from 1923.
Below: Herbert Smith with his young family in 1923.
George is on Herbert's knee.

and Italy. On his discharge, he went into partnership with his brother and father. During the late 30s the company had developed from jobbing builders into house builders, and in the post-war years a succession of Local Authority housing contracts were undertaken, and numerous private houses constructed. Bert and George carried on the business after Herbert's death in 1958, by which time mechanisation was on its way. Having bought a concrete mixer in the 1930s, they bought their first digger, a Whitlock, in 1959, and now the company has two JCB diggers and JCB forklifts with telescopic masts, capable of lifting three ton weights to a height of 36 feet. Their office has the latest computerised accounting and project management systems, CDM ✎ (Construction Design Management), a website, and a host of procedures to facilitate detailed record-keeping that Herbert would have shuddered to imagine.

Bert retired in 1970 and George in 1987. With John Smith as Managing Director and Alan as Contracts Director, H Smith and Sons have begun to diversify. In 1991 the company built a number of light industrial units and offices for rent on its Quarry Works site, and is currently developing an Antifire subsidiary specialising in building

materials that prevent the spread of fire. Meanwhile the list of satisfied customers keeps on growing - one of them being John Smith himself, whose home, a 200-year old corn mill on the edge of Honingham with a red brick house built onto the side, was created by the firm. The mill was covered in ivy and its roof and floor had collapsed; now, with new timbers, a new roof, a spiral staircase and re-plastered walls, it has become an attractive landmark which frequently arouses the curiosity of passing motorists.

H Smith and Sons (Honingham) Ltd pride themselves on being a small company capable of carrying out large contracts. Recently they have been engaged on a school extension contract at Gorleston worth half a million pounds, a million-pound contract for Peddars Way Housing Association, and a £280.000 total refurbishment of a depot at Cringleford.

Above: The present management. From left to right: Mr John E Smith, Mr George E Smith and Mr Alan GH Smith.
Top: The company's Dereham Road premises.
Left: Hand over of housing development at Middleton Crescent, Costersey to South Norfolk Council in 1980.

Skills that turn fantasy into reality

It is every architect's hope, when a cherished project nears fruition, that not only will the creation itself be appreciated and admired locally, but that the ideas and the planning which went into it will not end there, but will go on to become the inspiration for similar creations elsewhere. And this is exactly what happened when Norwich's Castle Mall shopping centre was opened; Michael Innes of Lambert Scott & Innes, the architects for the scheme, was approached by the Moscow City Government and invited to become involved in the design of a 400,000 square foot shopping centre on a site of world importance at Manezhnaya Square, adjoining the Kremlin and the Moscow State University.

Although this was, as far as we know, the first of Lambert Scott & Innes' projects to impress the Russian authorities, the firm has been designing buildings which have won the approval of people in this country since the establishment of the practice in its current form in 1971; but its history can be traced back through the two firms which combined in that year to form Lambert Scott & Innes: the partnership of Lambert & Innes, and the old-established firm of A F Scott

& Sons which had practised in Norwich since 1880.

Examples of A F Scott's early work survive in the form of various chapels and somewhat fragmented items of the industrial repertoire. During the war the firm was occupied by war damage scheduling and repair, and extensive defence work for the Admiralty, particularly at Laurence Scott's factories, but this too has now been demolished. The firm had by this time passed to

Above: Before and after Castle Mall - the old cattle market site. **Below:** *Castle Mall.*

Theo Scott, son of the founder, Augustus Frederic Scott; Theo Scott served on various committees concerned with post-war reconstruction, and was also President of the Norfolk and Norwich Association of Architects. His son John followed the family tradition, although he was commissioned in the Royal Navy during the war; his credits include the Hostel for the Young Deaf and restoration work at Muspole Street. By 1971 the firm of A F Scott & Sons was being run by John Scott, and Lambert & Innes by Christopher Lambert and Michael Innes; the former had previously practiced as Christopher Lambert & Partners and before that had worked in partnership with J Fletcher Watson.

J Fletcher Watson's contributions to local architecture include a number of well-known buildings, notably the

Above (both pictures): *The Norwich Playhouse.*
Right: *The Bank of Scotland.*

Bishop's Palace and the reconstruction of the Dolphin Inn in Heigham Street. Christopher Lambert himself was responsible for the Bank of Scotland in Queen Street, one of the shops on Timberhill, the conversion of Jarrolds Mill, St Luke's Church on Aylsham Road, and Norwich Playhouse. Michael Innes, with whom he formed a partnership in 1967, had designed extensions to Maddermarket Theatre in 1964, the headquarters of South Norfolk District Council, Mole Valley DCHQ in Dorking, won as the result of a competition, the BUPA hospitals in Norwich and Portsmouth, housing on Bracondale and in Pottergate and the conversion of Willow Lane Chapel into offices. A repertoire which began to set the style of the practice, which whilst remaining essentially Norwich based, has grown a reputation for winning work outside the region.

Following the amalgamation, the new firm of Lambert Scott & Innes continued to operate for a while from four small offices - A F Scott's original premises at Tombland, Lambert & Innes' original premises at Pull's Ferry, and additional branches at Princes Street and Thorpe Road. Having disposed of the four leases the firm then moved to a single large studio on the top floor

of 2 Dove Street. It was to remain here until the 1980s, when it moved to The Old Drill Hall in Cattle Market Street.

Benefiting from the combined talent and experience of these three distinguished architects and subsequently joined by David Ridel (creator of The Playhouse Bar) and David Thompson (responsible for The Norfolk Building, Norwich City College) the new practice was from the first destined to succeed, so the long list of credits which Lambert Scott & Innes has amassed will surprise no-one: retail schemes in Peterborough, Sutton Coldfield and Colchester, education projects for the East Norfolk Sixth Form College, Norwich School of Art and Norwich City College: leisure facilities from cinemas and theatres, to swimming pools and golf clubs, holiday chalets and even time share apartments; offices for both the public and the private sector, industrial units, warehouses and factories; hospital buildings and nursing homes; and housing schemes, again for both public and private sectors, ranging from luxury flats to an award-winning housing scheme for the frail elderly. The practice has won and been associated with a string of architectural awards including numerous Civic Trust Awards and Craftsmanship Awards, a Merton Design Award and a Civic Award; and one project alone has gained the RTPI Silver Jubilee Cup Planning Achievement,

the National Landscape Gold Award, the Business Commitment to the Environment Premier Award and the British Council of Shopping Centres New Centre Award . . . not to mention the admiration of the Russians!

Castle Mall Shopping Centre represents Lambert Scott & Innes' largest project to date. This £90 million scheme, carried out in conjunction with Bovis and Ove Arup & Partners, with Lambert Scott & Innes as lead consultants as well as architects, took some thirteen years to accomplish and posed some interesting challenges along the way. Their success in creating an attractive shopping complex with a floor area of around a million square feet, right underneath the Castle, lit from an amazing 100-yard long glasshouse roof and accessed by five separate and highly individual entrances, and all this without detracting from the views of the Castle, surpassed all expectations. Indeed, there were those who at the beginning were convinced that the entire scheme was 'a fantasy'. The fact that this fantasy has become reality is due in no small part to the ingenuity, the skill and the tenacity of Michael Innes, the partner who took responsibility for the project. It is also a reflection of this relatively small firm's flexibility and expertise in project management and in the advanced use of technology.

At the time of writing work on Castle Mall is still ongoing, and a 2,000 seat multi-screen cinema is yet to be added to the Timberhill end of the complex. Meanwhile Lambert Scott & Innes looks forward to being involved in many more innovative and varied projects, both in this country and abroad. Whatever the scale of the project, the firm will retain the personal culture of the medium-sized practice which is seldom found in large national firms. David Ridel, David Thompson and their team are currently contributing 'design' to the R G Carter 'design and build' elements of Riverside, now becoming visible next to Thorpe Station. It will continue to follow design principles which are sympathetic to context, appropriately combining innovative design with traditional features - and, now and again, enhancing reality with just a touch of fantasy!

Top left: Merchant's Court.
Top right: Housing at Bracondale.
Left: 37-39 Timberhill.

Stylish conveyances since the eighteenth century

Today, at the modern showrooms of Howes of Fakenham, you can inspect the latest Peugeot range. Around a hundred years ago, the same family firm had recently had on display a beautiful carriage which it had built on behalf of the citizens of Norwich, to be presented by them as a wedding gift to Princess Maud Victoria of Denmark, who had previously spent some years in Norfolk. This exquisite, carriage was painted in the royal colours of claret relieved with vermillion and beautifully varnished, and was upholstered in 'rich blue morocco cloth and silk lace', with large patent-leather wings to protect the occupants from mud splashes; it had rubber tyres, and the steps were lined with rubber to prevent slipping. The people of Norwich who came to view it were most impressed with the standard of workmanship, and Lord Suffield himself proclaimed it a perfect success. A contemporary report in the Norfolk Chronicle dated October 10th 1896 concluded that 'The firm are to be congratulated on showing the superior work that can be turned out in Norwich.'

Above: The coat of arms of Sir Andrew Buchanan, 1st Baronet 1807-1882, taken from his coach.
Below: The wedding gift to Princess Maud Victoria of Denmark from the people of Norfolk. This exquisite carriage was designed and built by the company.

Messrs Howes & Sons were quite accustomed to building coaches for Royalty, and over the years they were to supply no fewer than five carriages to Sandringham. Indeed, the origins of this firm's reputation for superior craftsmanship could be traced back over yet another hundred years to the late 18th century, when it was trading as coach and harness makers at St George's, Colegate, where it had been established in 1784 by a Mr William Spratt. The business moved to Chapel Field in 1796, and in 1861 its name was changed to Howes & Sons.

A fascinating memento of the firm's early days as carriage builders can be seen adorning the walls of the registered office. In the early 19th century it was the custom of the gentry to have their coat of arms or family crest hand-painted on the carriage, on small panels. When a gentleman took delivery of a new carriage he would invariably ask the company to break up the old one, and the coachman would ask to have the old panel cut out as a souvenir (see above). At the end of World War II twelve of these panels were still awaiting collection, and the company decided that as the chances of anyone coming forward to claim them at this stage were so remote, it would be appropriate to take them out of their box and put them on display at its offices.

Howes & Sons Ltd was incorporated under the Companies Act on 8 March 1913, and its first chairman was Stanley Howes, the father of the present chairman. Born on 12th July 1874 in a house in Chapel Field attached to the business premises, Stanley Howes was also a director of Boulton and Paul Ltd at Riverside Road, and became vice-chairman of the British Wire Netting Association. He was an exceptionally skillful engineer, and one of his achievements at Boulton and Paul was the construction of the framework of the R101 Airship. This airship unfortunately crashed at Beauvais in northern France on 5th October 1930, but it was made clear at the official inquiry that no blame for the crash was attached to the work undertaken by Boulton and Paul.

Howes & Sons became the original Wolseley agents for Norfolk from the turn of the 20th century, and the business carried on growing; a major branch was opened at St George's Street, Ipswich, when the firm was appointed Rootes main dealers, and Howes & Sons continued to trade from there for many decades, transferring their franchise from Rootes to Talbot, and subsequently becoming a Peugeot dealership before selling the premises in 1986.

Jack Wyndham Howes, the present chairman of the company and an active member of the board, first became a director in 1939. He became interested in motoring at a very early age, and as a schoolboy one of

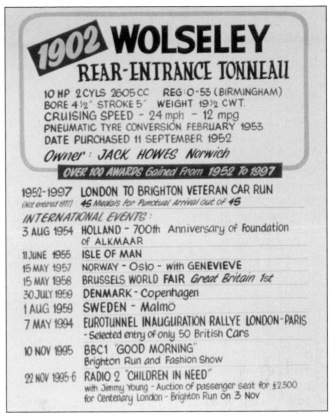

1902 WOLSELEY
REAR-ENTRANCE TONNEAU
10 HP 2 CYLS 2605 CC   REG: O-53 (BIRMINGHAM)
BORE 4½" STROKE 5" WEIGHT 19½ CWT.
CRUISING SPEED - 24 mph - 12 mpg
PNEUMATIC TYRE CONVERSION FEBRUARY 1953
DATE PURCHASED 11 SEPTEMBER 1952
Owner: JACK HOWES Norwich

OVER 100 AWARDS Gained From 1952 To 1997

1952-1997	LONDON TO BRIGHTON VETERAN CAR RUN
(Not entered 1977)	*45 Medals for Punctual Arrival out of 45*

INTERNATIONAL EVENTS:

3 AUG 1954	HOLLAND - 700th Anniversary of Foundation of ALKMAAR
11 JUNE 1955	ISLE OF MAN
15 MAY 1957	NORWAY - Oslo - with GENEVIEVE
15 MAY 1958	BRUSSELS WORLD FAIR *Great Britain 1st*
30 JULY 1959	DENMARK - Copenhagen
1 AUG 1959	SWEDEN - Malmö
7 MAY 1994	EUROTUNNEL INAUGURATION RALLYE LONDON - PARIS - *Selected entry of only 50 British Cars*
10 NOV 1995	BBC1 'GOOD MORNING' Brighton Run and Fashion Show
22 NOV 1995-6	RADIO 2 'CHILDREN IN NEED' with Jimmy Young - Auction of passenger seat for £2,300 for Centenary London - Brighton Run On 3 Nov

his great passions was to 'do' the London to Brighton Run. Two of the regular participants in this event are Wolseley cars with Howes coachwork dated not later than 1904, and ever since the early 1950s Jack's own 1902 Wolseley 10 hp, with the registration number O-53, has become a familiar sight on the Run. Jack saw the car advertised in The Autocar in 1952 and bought it with his Army gratuity, and since then it has become something of a star in its own right. Not only does it hold the record for successfully completing the London to Brighton Run - to date Jack has entered it in the rally 45 times and completed successfully on every single occasion - but O-53 was also one of the cars selected to take part in the official opening ceremony of the

Eurotunnel on 7th May 1994, performed by the Queen and President Mitterand and featuring 50 cars from each nation.

Another of Jack's cars which has brought him into the limelight is a 20 hp Rolls-Royce Doctor's coupé, which was one of the 17 cars chosen to represent Great Britain on the maiden voyage of the QE2 on 2nd May 1969.

In 1953 Stanley Howes invited Mr B W H Nurse FCA to join the board of directors, and from that time on he worked closely with Jack Howes in running the firm. Since 1954 the business has operated through its subsidiary and associated companies in Norwich, Woodbridge and Fakenham. At present Mr Michael Downes and Mr Colin Humphries are actively engaged in the day-to-day management of the company; Mr Michael Downes became associated with the company in November 1959, working at Chapel Field, and Mr Colin Humphries, Mr Nurse's son-in-law, joined in 1971. Mr Humphries was responsible for establishing a new dealership at Mile Cross Lane which was opened in 1973. Unfortunately a disastrous fire occurred there in 1980; the premises were rebuilt, but sadly many of the company's old records were destroyed. Subsequently the new buildings at Norwich Road, Fakenham were established under Colin Humphries' direction, and at the present time Howes of Fakenham holds the Peugeot main dealership for North Norfolk at the modern Fakenham premises, under the direction of Mr Colin Humphries and Mr Michael Downes.

Above: Some of the many events attended by Jack Howes' Wolseley.
Above left: Jack Howes boarding the plane at Lympne near Hythe, Kent for Le Touquet-Paris-Plage Aéroport in the late 1950s.

The town within the city

Shopping centres have become an integral part of city commerce, and Norwich is fortunate in enjoying the shopping facilities offered by Anglia Square - a precinct which was originally developed some thirty years ago, when it was seen as a tremendous boost to the then near-derelict Magdalen Street area, and which has not been afraid to change with the times so as to continue to offer shoppers an interesting range of shops situated in an attractive environment.

The opening of Anglia Square in August 1970 was the culmination of much careful planning and some five years of construction work, and the thought which went into its design has reaped rewards, with many of the features built into the centre remaining to this day crucial factors in the centre's success.

One vital advantage is that Anglia Square was sited so as to make it easily accessible to motorists, with ample car parking available in the adjoining multi-storey car park. Since 1970 the city's traffic has increased tremendously, but the one-way traffic system which has been introduced conveniently guides the motorist to Magdalen Street without touching the city centre.

Another major factor in Anglia Square's continued success lies in its range of stores and leisure facilities. Over the years big names in Anglia Square have included the Odeon,

Sainsburys, Fine Fare, Roys of Wroxham, Maple furniture company and the discount store QD. Some of these businesses have remained there throughout, and some have gone, to be replaced by equally popular outlets. Traders like Anglia Square; the opening of Roys Variety Store in 1996 marked Roys' return to the Square after six years' absence, and QD's expansion in 1995 took it from smaller premises inside the Square to a new store, twice the size, which formed part of the Square's revamped frontage.

Other improvements over the years include extra security, with CCTV combined with 'village bobby' style patrols; attractive landscaping; and a variety of community initiatives and attractions, often with local charity involvement.

Hailed when new Centre Manager Roy Ruggles took over in 1996 as 'a town within a city', Anglia Square has continued to cultivate a family-friendly atmosphere, investing as necessary to maintain a pleasant shopping environment for the enjoyment of the community which it serves. Today, competition with Norwich's other shopping facilities is keen, but this easily-accessible shopping centre continues enjoy well-deserved popularity as a fun and safe place for the family.

Above: *The advertisement from when the Square was 're-vamped' in 1995.*
Below: *Street entertainment in Anglia Square.*

A true family concern that has been a sparkling success for 70 years

When Charlie Hannant founded the Hannant family business back in 1929, his main aim was to provide for his wife and children. As it turns out, the business has gone on to provide for his grand-children, his great-grandchildren, his great-great-grand-children . . . and, hopefully, many generations of Hannants yet to come!

To begin with, window cleaning was just one of the domestic services which Charlie Hannant provided; he would also chop wood, deliver kindling, and paint door knockers for a penny a time. But window cleaning proved the most reliable source of income, with larger contracts such as cleaning the windows of Blythe Jex School in Sprowston Road in preparation for the school's opening, after the builders had finished. Hannants remained a one-man concern until 1945, when Charlie's son Alfred was planning his future after coming out of the Air Force. Alfred could have joined the Metropolitan Police, but after being away from Norwich for six years he wanted to spend some time at home. So Charlie took him into partnership, and together the two men worked hard and built up their business; and in 1961 they were joined by Alfred's son David.

The chief problem faced by window cleaners in the days before central heating was that during the bad winters, such as the one in 1962, windows used to stay frozen up for weeks on end; and this left them unable to work. It was David who decided that the way round this problem was to work inside as well as out, and preliminary enquiries among the firms whose windows they cleaned showed a great demand for office cleaning services. Alfred decided to leave it to the younger generation to start this new venture, so David and his wife Jenny set themselves the challenge of building up David M Hannant Cleaning Services. This they did so successfully that by 1980 they were employing a dozen staff; by 1990 this had risen to around 60, and today the firm has some 104 full and part-time employees. Their success lies in providing a reliable, personal service which customers are happy with; many of their contracts have been ongoing for 30 years or more, and their oldest client is the original Stewart & Pattersons Brewery which has retained their services through numerous owners and alterations for 70 years.

With David and Jenny's daughter Rachel Smith in charge of wages and their son Kevin a partner in the business, customers can rest assured that nothing can take the shine off the service provided by Hannants - a true family concern.

Top left: *Charlie Hannant (wearing cap) is pictured with his son Alfred and his four daughters outside the original premises on Shipstone Road, Norwich in 1936.*
Below: *David and Kevin's office at 306A, Dereham Road, home to their company since 1988.*

The Tombland Fair in a picture dating from almost 50 years ago.

Acknowledgments

Diane Yeadon and Mr Clive Jones, Local Studies Librarian at the Norfolk Studies Library, Gildengate House; Mrs S.J Scholey and colleagues, Women's Royal Voluntary Service; R.C Snelling Limited; T. Gill & Son (Norwich) Limited; Mr R. Scott and the unsung heroes at the marvellous Horsham St. Faith Aviation Museum; The staff at Norfolk Record Office for permission to reproduce material from the Central Office of Information collection; Mr A. Adcock, Hon. Sec. Norwich 1st Scouts; Sub Officer Richard Smith, Norwich Fire Brigade Headquarters; Mr Richard Auton, City Hall Norwich, for permission to use images originating from Norwich City Council departments, and Sue Garrod, Norwich Community Health Partnership.

*Thanks are also due to
Andrew Mitchell who penned the editorial text
and Margaret Wakefield and Mike Kirke for their copywriting skills*